wasatch wildflowers

steve hegji

wasatch wildflowers

steve hegji

CFI,
Springville, UT

ISBN 13:978-1-59955-382-5

Published by CFI, an imprint of Cedar Fort, Inc., 2373 W. 700 S., Springville, UT 84663
Distributed by Cedar Fort, Inc., www.cedarfort.com

LIBRARY OF CONGRESS CATALOGING-IN-PUBLICATION DATA

Library of Congress Cataloging-in-Publication Data

Hegji, Steve.
  Wasatch wildflowers / Steve Hegji.
    p. cm.
  Includes bibliographical references and index.
  ISBN 978-1-59955-382-5 (acid-free paper)
  1. Wild flowers--Wasatch Range (Utah and Idaho)--Identification. I. Title.

QK189.H44 2010
582.1309792'2--dc22

2009046096

Cover and page design by Angela D. Olsen
Cover design © 2010 by Lyle Mortimer
Edited by Heidi Doxey

Printed in China

10 9 8 7 6 5 4 3 2 1

Printed on acid-free paper

Dedication

TO PETE
who is with me in the high places.

AND TO PATTI
who is with me in all places, forever.

Acknowledgments

My heartfelt thanks to these wonderful folks:

Al Schneider (swcoloradowildflowers.com) came along at a time when I was struggling to identify wildflowers and just finding out it could be difficult. He taught me it was even more complex than I thought but helped me climb the learning curve. He kindly reviewed some of my early writing and continues to help with wildflower identification.

Stan Welsh (A Utah Flora) continues to help me identify the plants I photograph by donating his precious time, books, and vegetables. I wish I'd met him forty years ago.

Bill Gray also reviewed portions of this book and continues to act as a sounding board for identification.

Greg Witt (Alpenwild.com) first suggested that the combination of my photographs and the effort I had put into identifying them would make a book. He found the publisher for me! After all that, how could I refuse? He's a great hiking companion.

Jennifer Fielding, acquisitions editor from Cedar Fort, Inc., who is one of the nicest people I've ever worked with and who did a wonderful job nurturing a first-time author.

Heidi Doxey, editor for Cedar Fort Inc., who smoothly and uncomplainingly edited the book. It can't be easy editing a book like this, especially when you toss in the enormous index that I asked her to build. I hope you think of her every time you find it easy to look up a plant name in any of a variety of ways.

Angela Olsen, graphic designer from Cedar Fort, Inc., who took my material and turned it into a great looking book. I hope you'll all agree.

Contents

"Consider the lilies of the field. . . even Solomon in
all his glory was not arrayed like one of these."

Matthew 6:28–29

INTRODUCTION

All wildflowers are beautiful. In some cases the beauty may not be apparent until you get very close, but it's there nonetheless. The purpose of this book is to get you excited about that beauty and to teach you how to see the plants in a different way.

Most of us wildflower enthusiasts start out by looking at a flower; reacting to the pleasing color, shape, or fragrance; and then wanting to put a name to it. You'll find as you read this book that there are lots of characteristics that define a wildflower species. You'll take this new knowledge with you into the field and begin noticing other aspects. How do the leaves look from the base up to the tip? What is their shape, size, and arrangement? Do they have veins, toothed edges, sticky, or hairy surfaces? And the flowers—are they single or in clusters? Are there ray and disk flowers in a single head? Do they have both petals and sepals? Are the flowers hairy? Do they have colored patches or spots?

As your powers of observation increase, so will the pleasure you take in the beauty and wonder of God's creation.

"What's in a name? that which we call a rose
By any other name would smell as sweet;"

Romeo and Juliet, William Shakespeare, 1594

PLANT NAMES

During a field trip with a friend, we stopped to photograph a Yellow Salsify flower. My friend remarked that he'd grown up calling it a "milkweed." Salsify does have a milky juice in the stems and leaves; it is one of many such plants within the Sunflower family. But there is also a separate plant family known as Milkweed. If we hadn't been standing in front of the plant itself, we would have had some difficulty agreeing on what we were talking about. A third person who only knew it as "Goatsbeard" would not have understood either of us.

This example illustrates that common names for plants lack precision and standardization. The same plant can, and often does, have many different common names.

The scientific name for a species is composed of a unique combination of genus and species, often derived from Latin or Greek words. Yellow Salsify has the generic name, *Tragopogon,* and the specific epithet, *dubius*; thus, its scientific name is *Tragopogon dubius*. This name is unique and standard throughout the world. Be aware, however, that scientific names can change as new data is acquired or more studies done. There is often a transition period, decades long, that determines whether or not taxonomists will accept the new name.

You'll find both the common name and the scientific name—multiples of each if applicable—in this book. The common names are easier for beginners to remember and are often descriptive (Stonecrop, for example). The scientific names are what you'll need if you decide to do further research. These names have all been placed in the Index to make it easier to find each flower in the book.

Just for the record, the primary common and scientific names used in this book have been taken from *A Utah Flora* by Stan Welsh (see References on page 207). This is the most comprehensive treatment of Utah flora available today. However, I do not follow *A Utah Flora* for five plant family names. Instead I have chosen to use a ruling from the 1992 International Code of Botanical Nomenclature for the following families:

Brassicaceae (Mustard)

Asteraceae (Sunflower/Aster/Composite)

Lamiaceae (Mint)

Fabaceae (Pea)

Apiaceae (Parsley/Carrot)

BOTANICAL LANGUAGE

Like all serious scientific disciplines, botany has its own language. This language is compact and precise. If you wanted to say, "the leaves on the stem, as opposed to those at the base, where the plant comes out of the ground," you would just use the botanical word "cauline." However, most of us don't know or use these words, and I've tried to avoid them as much as possible. The few that I do use are defined in a glossary at the back of the book.

For those of you who want to delve further, I highly recommend *Plant Identification Terminology, An Illustrated Glossary* by James and Melinda Harris (see References on page 207). I could not have gotten very far reading or using a botanical key without this wonderful book!

HOW TO USE THIS BOOK

The book is organized by flower color, and you'll see little colored tabs on every page, marking each section. In most cases this should get you into the correct section quickly. However, be aware that some flowers may look pink to me, but red or purple to you, and you'll occasionally have to look in other sections.

Yellow, white, and purple are the most common colors and make up the majority of the flower pages. For these sections I've put the flowers that are daisy-like in appearance first. On the pages for these flowers you'll see a little daisy graphic imbedded in the colored tab.

Within the color and shape organization, the pages are organized by scientific family name. For example, in the White, nondaisy-like section, Cow Parsnip comes first because it is a member of the Apiaceae family. It is followed by Pearly Everlasting, a member of the Asteraceae family. I've organized them by family because as you learn about one plant thoroughly, you'll find that it helps you recognize other plants of the same family. Soon you'll reach a stage where you'll see a plant and think "that plant must be in the Pea family (Fabaceae)," and quickly be able to turn to the Pea family pages for that color.

Both the pictures and text found on each page are for your edification and enjoyment. I chose beautiful pictures that would help you identify the plant. The associated text is obviously not comprehensive, nor could it be in this format. But it should be helpful to you when confirming your visual identification of a plant.

The JFMAMJJASOND symbol found on the bottom edge of the picture on each flower page represents the twelve months of the year. The lighter green portions depict the range of months in which I have usually seen the plant in bloom. Depending on weather and location, you may see the plant in flower outside these time frames.

The vertical ruler symbol shown in the middle of the page, at the outside edge, represents the maximum height of the plant based on herbarium specimens. Most plants that you observe will be somewhat shorter, although occasionally you'll come across a specimen as tall, or taller. One further convention requires explanation. I have used a non-botanical set of terms to describe the elevation-dependent zones associated with each plant's habitat. Low elevation roughly translates to less than 6000′, moderate elevation to 6000–8000′, and high elevation above 8000′.

This book is the beginning of a great adventure for you. I know you'll come to love the beautiful plants of the Wasatch Front.

Steve Hegji, March 2010

Flower Symbol Legend

COMMON NAME
(Scientific Name)
Family (Scientific Family Name)

 FLOWERS

 FRUIT

 LEAVES

 HABITAT

 RANGE

 ADDITIONAL INFORMATION

JFMAMJJASOND **FLOWERING MONTHS**

 MAXIMUM HEIGHT

ROSE HEATH
(*Chaetopappa ericoides*)
Sunflower Family (Asteraceae)

JFMAMJJASOND

Rose Heath *is a cheerful, springtime addition to the drier areas in the valleys and foothills of the Wasatch Front. It tends to grow in patches that are covered with small, white daisies.*

 Up to ½″ across, 12–25 white ray flowers, yellow disk flowers.

 Up to ½″, straight, stiff hair on the edges and upper leaves lying along the stem.

 Desert shrub and Pinyon/Juniper communities; low to moderate elevations.

 Most Utah counties; south-central and southwestern US.

 Ericoides means "resembling Erica." *Ericaceae* is the family name for "heath," which in Utah includes huckleberry and manzanita. Rose Heath is not a true heath, but its leaves resemble some species of heath.

 Up to 7″

1

SPREADING DAISY
(*Erigeron divergens*)
Sunflower Family (Asteraceae)

J F M A M J J A S O N D

Spreading Daisy *produces numerous spreading branches, hence the common name. They are cute little flowers—often pinkish as a bud, becoming white when fully open. You should be able to find them on a brushy hillside trail.*

Up to
20″

 Up to 1″ across, 75–150 white, pinkish, or purplish rays, yellow disk flowers.

 Basal leaves up to 3″, spatula shaped or reverse lance shaped, cauline leaves much smaller.

 Sagebrush, mountain brush, and forest communities; low to high elevations.

 All Utah counties; central and western North America.

 Divergens means "spreading out widely from the center."

Other Names:
Spreading Fleabane

2

VERNAL DAISY
(Erigeron pumilus)
Sunflower Family (Asteraceae)

JFMAMJJASOND

Vernal Daisy is possibly the most common Erigeron in Utah. It has beautifully symmetrical flowers with numerous, slender, white rays and a big, rounded yellow disk. The leaves, stems, and flower heads are covered with short white hair.

 Up to 1½″ across, 50–100 white, pink, or bluish-purple rays, yellow disk flowers.

 Basal leaves up to 3″, narrowly spatula shaped or reverse lance-shaped, cauline leaves typically smaller.

 Desert shrub, sagebrush, mountain brush communities; low to high elevations.

 Most Utah counties; southwestern US.

 Pumilus means "dwarf." *Concinnus,* one of the other species names, means "neat, elegant." The major difference between Vernal Daisy and Spreading Daisy on the previous page is that Spreading Daisy grows from a taproot, while Vernal Daisy is a perennial and has a woody base.

Up to 20″

Other Names:

Navajo Fleabane

Erigeron concinnus

ROCKSLIDE DAISY
(*Erigeron leiomerus*)
Sunflower Family (Asteraceae)

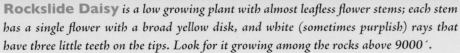

JFMAMJJASOND

Rockslide Daisy *is a low growing plant with almost leafless flower stems; each stem has a single flower with a broad yellow disk, and white (sometimes purplish) rays that have three little teeth on the tips. Look for it growing among the rocks above 9000´.*

Up to 6˝

 Up to 1˝ across, 15–60 white, or bluish-purple ray flowers, yellow disk flowers.

 Basal leaves up to 3˝, spatula shaped or reverse lance shaped, cauline leaves few and small.

 Talus slopes, boulder fields, and meadows in pine and alpine communities; high elevations.

 Wasatch Front and Uintah mountains; CO, ID, MT, NM, NV, WY.

 The ray flowers start out very small, narrow, and pointed, and then expand greatly as they reach full bloom. Many species of *Erigeron* will show this same growth pattern.

Other Names:

Glaber Daisy

4

ENGELMANN'S ASTER
(*Aster engelmannii*)
Sunflower Family (Asteraceae)

J F M A M J J A S O N D

Engelmann's Aster *is often seen as a grouping of tall, curving stems; topped with a cluster of graceful, white, daisy-like flowers. Look for it along the edges of mountain trails.*

 Typically in clusters of many flowers; each white flower up to 2″ across.

 Up to 6″ long, lance shaped or elliptical.

 Mountain brush and forest communities; moderate to high elevations.

 Northern Utah counties; western North America.

Engelmannii is named after George Engelmann (1809–84) a botanist from St. Louis. The Engelmann Spruce, which the early Utah settlers called White Pine, is also named after him.

Other Names:
Aster elegans
Eucephalus engelmannii

Up to 5′

5

COW PARSNIP
(*Heracleum lanatum*)
Parsley Family (Apiaceae)

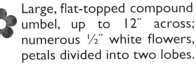
JFMAMJJASOND

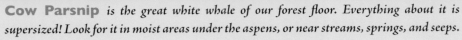
Cow Parsnip *is the great white whale of our forest floor. Everything about it is supersized! Look for it in moist areas under the aspens, or near streams, springs, and seeps.*

Up to 8′

Large, flat-topped compound umbel, up to 12″ across; numerous ½″ white flowers, petals divided into two lobes.

Up to 14″ long and broad, oval in outline, divided into 3 lobes, each lobe again divided and toothed.

Stream sides, wet meadows, and Aspen communities; low to moderate elevations.

Mountainous Utah counties; most of North America.

Lanatum means ″covered with long, woolly hair.″ Native Americans used this plant for food and medicine.

Other Names:
Heracleum maximum
Heracleum sphondylium

PEARLY EVERLASTING
(*Anaphalis margaritacea*)
Sunflower Family (Asteraceae)

JFMAMJJASOND

Pearly Everlasting *is here in the white flowers section of the book because the most noticeable feature of the flower is the pure white bracts, which are mesmerizing in their purity and intensity.*

 Small ¼″ flowers arranged in large, flat-topped clusters. Each individual flower is surrounded by a series of white, overlapping bracts. The flower contains only tiny yellow disk flowers.

 Lance-shaped leaves up to 5″ long, alternating up the flower stalk, which is white with a thick covering of short hair.

 Meadows, stream banks, road sides, and open forest communities; low to high elevations.

 Northern half of the Wasatch Front; most of North America.

 Anaphalis is from the Greek word for a similar plant. *Margaritacea* is from the Latin word for "pearl."

Other Names:

Gnaphalium margaritaceum

Up to 2′

7

COMMON PUSSYTOES
(*Antennaria parvifolia*)
Sunflower Family (Asteraceae)

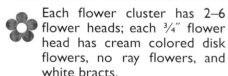

J F M A M J J A S O N D

Common Pussytoes *has white fuzzy looking flowers and soft gray-green leaves that appear to have a white margin near the tip.*

Up to 6"

Each flower cluster has 2–6 flower heads; each ¾" flower head has cream colored disk flowers, no ray flowers, and white bracts.

Basal leaves are up to 1½" long and spade shaped; cauline leaves are straight and slender.

Sagebrush, forest, and alpine meadow communities; low to high elevations.

Most Utah counties; western US; Canada

Antennaria means "antenna," in reference to the appearance of the male flowers. *Parvifolia* means "small-leaved." Don't confuse Pussytoes with Pearly Everlasting on the previous page—Pearly Everlasting is much taller and does not form a mat of basal leaves (shown in the left inset).

Second Species: Rosy Pussytoes (*Antennaria microphylla*), shown in the right inset, has pink-tipped bracts.

8

FILFOIL YARROW
(*Achillea millefolium*)
Sunflower Family (Asteraceae)

J F M A M J J A S O N D

You'll run into this ubiquitous plant wherever you go in the summer. The numerous white flowers and finely divided leaves give **Filfoil Yarrow** *a delicate appearance. It has a pleasant fragrance and dries well.*

 A flat or slightly rounded inflorescence consisting of numerous small white (sometimes pink) flower heads; ray and disk flowers present in each flower head.

 Up to 10″ long, each leaf divided into many small, slender leaflets.

 Brush, forest, and alpine communities; low to high elevations.

 All Utah; northern hemisphere.

 Achillea is named for Achilles, who supposedly used this plant on the wounds of his soldiers. It has been used for medicinal purposes in the past. *Millefolium* means "a thousand leaves" and refers to the many leaflets of each leaf.

Other Names:
Common Yarrow
Milfoil Yarrow

Up to 3 ½′

9

DOUGLAS' DUSTYMAIDEN
(*Chaenactis douglasii*)
Sunflower Family (Asteraceae)

JFMAMJJASOND

Douglas' Dustymaiden *has fern-like leaves, and a globular flower head densely packed with white or pink disk flowers.*

Up to 2′

 Loose clusters of several white to pink flowers, up to 1½″ across; disk flowers only, no ray flowers.

 Compound, up to 3″, divided 1–3 times into parallel rows of small leaflets.

 Brush and forest communities; low to high elevations.

 All Utah counties; western North America.

 Chaenactis is derived from two Greek words and means "gaping ray," and refers to broad opening of the disk flowers. *Douglasii* is named after David Douglas (1798–1834), a Scotsman who discovered many plants, including the Douglas Fir, which Utah pioneers called Red Pine.

Other Names: Pincushion Flower, Bride's Bouquet, False Yarrow.

Second Species: Alpine Dustymaiden (*Chaenactis alpinum*), is very similar in appearance to Douglas' Dustymaiden but is only 4″ tall, and in Utah is only found above 9800′.

10

TASSELFLOWER
(*Brickellia grandiflora*)
Sunflower Family (Asteraceae)

JFMAMJJASOND

Tasselflower can be hard to spot because its abundant foliage tends to hide the downward hanging, pale flowers. The flower clusters are very attractive and it's a plant worth looking for.

 Cream colored, ½″ head of disk flowers, no ray flowers.

 Up to 4″ long, generally heart shaped, and serrated.

Rocky hillsides in mountain brush communities; moderate to high elevations.

 Most Utah counties; western North America.

 Brickellia is named after Dr. John Brickell (1749–1809), a naturalist and physician in Georgia. *Grandiflora* means "large flowered."

Other Names:
Brickellbush
Coleosanthus grandiflorus

Up to
3′

DWARF CRYPTANTHA
(*Cryptantha humilis*)
Borage Family (Boraginaceae)

JFMAMJJASOND

Dwarf Cryptantha *has white, bouquet-like clusters of flowers and numerous hairy leaves. Look for it on dry sites and rocky hillsides.*

Up to 12"

 Rounded cylindrical cluster; white flowers, up to ¼" across, 5 lobes, yellowish rim in the center.

 Up to 2", spatula or reverse lance shaped, variously hairy.

 Most Utah counties; western US.

 Most Utah counties; south-central and southwestern US.

 Cryptantha is derived from two Greek words and means "hidden flower," which obviously does not apply to this species. *Humilis* means "low growing, humble." There are about 10 species of Cryptantha found on the Wasatch Front, and about 60 species in all of Utah.

Other Names:

Low Cryptantha
Roundspike Cryptantha

12

PALE STICKSEED
(*Hackelia patens*)
Borage Family (Boraginaceae)

JFMAMJJASOND

Pale Stickseed *has a light, open appearance with numerous white flowers in clusters. The petals are tinged at the base with blue or purple. The flowering stem elongates in a graceful curve, and the nutlets hang down below it.*

 Each plant usually has many flower clusters; each cluster has many white, ¼″ flowers with 5 petals having a pair of blue or purple stripes at the base, and a white and yellow center.

 Up to 6″ long, slender, and pointed.

 Sagebrush and forest communities; low to high elevations.

 Most counties of Utah; OR, ID, MT, WY, NV.

 Hackelia is named after Josef Hackel (1783–1869) a Czech botanist. *Patens* means "spreading," in reference to the growth habit of the plant. Look for Pale Stickseed to bloom about one month before its two blue colored cousins, Showy and Small-flowered Stickseed.

Other Names:
Spotted Stickseed
Spotted Forget-Me-Not

Up to
3′

HEARTLEAF BITTERCRESS
(*Cardamine cordifolia*)
Mustard Family (Brassicaceae)

JFMAMJJASOND

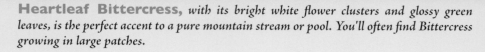

Heartleaf Bittercress, *with its bright white flower clusters and glossy green leaves, is the perfect accent to a pure mountain stream or pool. You'll often find Bittercress growing in large patches.*

Up to
2 ½'

 Hemispherical cluster of white flowers; each flower up to 1", with 4 petals.

 Up to 3" long, almost as broad, heart shaped, with irregularly shaped broad serrations.

 Stream banks and seeps in forest communities; low to high elevations.

 Most Utah counties; western North America.

 Cardamine is derived from the Greek word for cress plants. *Cordifolia* means "heart-shaped leaves."

JFMAMJJASOND

Red Elderberry *is a large, robust shrub with large, serrated leaves and a rounded cone-shaped cluster of tiny white flowers.*

 Rounded conical cluster composed of numerous 1/4" creamy-white flowers.

 Rounded cluster of inedible red berries.

 Each leaf has rows of 5–7 leaflets; leaflets up to 6" long, serrated.

 Forest and grass communities; moderate to high elevations.

 Most Utah counties; most of North America.

Second Species: Blue Elderberry (*Sambucus caerulea*) has large clusters of an edible blue fruit covered with a whitish film. It is taller than Red Elderberry and has larger, flat-topped flower clusters.

Other Names:

Sambucus microbotrys
   (for Red Elderberry)
Sambucus nigra
   (for Blue Elderberry)

Up to 6′

15

JAMES' CHICKWEED
(*Stellaria jamesiana*)
Pink Family (Caryophyllaceae)

JFMAMJJASOND

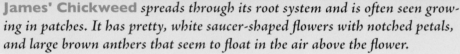

James' Chickweed *spreads through its root system and is often seen growing in patches. It has pretty, white saucer-shaped flowers with notched petals, and large brown anthers that seem to float in the air above the flower.*

Up to
2′

White, up to 1″; 5 petals divided into 2 lobes; flower head covered with glandular spots.

Up to 6″ long, opposite pairs, lance shaped and pointed, with tiny glandular spots.

Brush, and forest communities; low to high elevations.

All Utah counties; most of North America.

Jamesiana is named for Edwin James, a surgeon, botanist, and explorer. He was part of the federal government's Yellowstone expedition that explored the Rocky Mountains.

Other Names:

Tuber Starwort
Pseudostellaria jamesiana
Arenaria jamesiana

DOUGLAS' CAMPION
(*Silene douglasii*)
Pink Family (Caryophyllaceae)

JFMAMJJASOND

Colored flowers are spectacular, but there is something especially attractive about a flower that is pure white. **Douglas' Campion,** *with its pure white petals divided into two lobes and its inflated and striped flower head, is a beauty.*

 White, up to 1½", 5 petals divided into 2 lobes; flower head inflated, papery, and with purplish or greenish stripes.

 Cauline leaves up to 3", lance shaped or elliptical, hairy; basal leaves withered at flowering time.

 Brush and forest communities; moderate to high elevations.

 Wasatch Front; western US, excluding the southwest states.

Second Species: Menzies' Campion (*Silene menziesii*), shown in the inset, is very similar to Douglas' Campion but has smaller flowers, and the flower heads are not striped, inflated, and papery.

Other Names:

Douglas' Catchfly
  (for Douglas' Campion)
Menzies' Catchfly
  (for Menzies' Campion)

Up to 2½'

17

RED-OSIER DOGWOOD
(Cornus sericea)
Dogwood Family (Cornaceae)

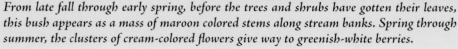

JFMAMJJASOND

From late fall through early spring, before the trees and shrubs have gotten their leaves, this bush appears as a mass of maroon colored stems along stream banks. Spring through summer, the clusters of cream-colored flowers give way to greenish-white berries.

Up to 12´

 Small cream-colored flowers in a flat cluster about 3˝ across

 Green, becoming white, pea-sized berries.

 Oval or lance-shaped deciduous leaves 1–8˝ long. Green on top but pale-colored underneath.

 Streambanks and other moist sites; low to high elevations.

 All Utah counties; North America.

 Deer browse on this plant

Other Names:
Kinnikinik
Red-twig Dogwood
American Dogwood
Cornus stolonifera

18

CASE'S CORYDALIS
(*Corydalis caseana*)
Fumitory Family (Fumariaceae)

J F M A M J J A S O N D

Case's Corydalis is a large, fast growing plant with multiple compound leaves, and a dense flower cluster. The flowers are very unusual. Make sure to take a close look!

 Long spiky cluster, 50–200 white or pinkish flowers; one of the petals forming a spur behind the corolla, two other purple-tipped petals fused together over the top of the stigma.

 Large compound leaf, with elliptical or oblong leaflets.

 Stream banks or moist sites in forest communities; moderate to high elevations.

 Salt Lake, Utah, Wasatch, and Weber counties; CA, CO, ID, NM, OR, WA.

 Case's Corydalis is poisonous to livestock. The dry seed pods will spring open when touched.

Other Names:
Case's Fitweed
Sierra Fumewort

Up to 3 ½'

19

RICHARDSON'S GERANIUM
(Geranium richardsonii)
Geranium Family (Geraniaceae)

J F M A M J J A S O N D

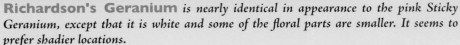

Richardson's Geranium *is nearly identical in appearance to the pink Sticky Geranium, except that it is white and some of the floral parts are smaller. It seems to prefer shadier locations.*

Up to 4′

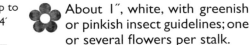 About 1″, white, with greenish or pinkish insect guidelines; one or several flowers per stalk.

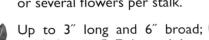 Up to 3″ long and 6″ broad; divided into 5–7 large lobes, each divided into smaller lobes.

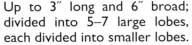 Sagebrush, mountain brush, forest communities; low to high elevations.

 Most Utah counties; western North America.

 Richardsonii is named after Sir John Richardson (1787–1865), an Artic explorer and a man of many other accomplishments.

20

HORSE-NETTLE
(*Agastache urticifolia*)
Mint Family (Lamiaceae)

JFMAMJJASOND

This tall member of the mint family has fragrant leaves and large clusters of small white flowers with pink bracts. The flower head is equally beautiful whether the flowers have opened or not.

 Cylindrical flower cluster up to 6˝ long, white flowers up to ½˝, with pink bracts.

 Up to 3˝ long, oval or almost triangular, serrated, in pairs all the way up the stem.

 Sagebrush and forest communities from middle to high elevations.

 Central and western Utah counties; western US, excluding AZ and NM.

 Agastache means "like an ear of corn or wheat." *Urticifolia* means "having nettle-like leaves." It's important you learn to recognize this plant; it's a joy to walk through, whereas Stinging Nettle is not!

Other Names:
Nettleleaf Giant Hyssop
Nettleleaf Horsemint

Up to 6´

21

SEGO LILY
(*Calochortus nuttallii*)
Lily Family (Liliaceae)

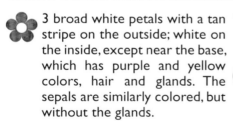

JFMAMJJASOND

Sego Lily *is the state flower of Utah. Look for it in the foothills, hiding in the grasses, around the beginning of June. The white flower is very beautiful and intricate on the inside.*

Up to 20˝

3 broad white petals with a tan stripe on the outside; white on the inside, except near the base, which has purple and yellow colors, hair and glands. The sepals are similarly colored, but without the glands.

Usually 3 narrow leaves, up to 4˝ long.

Grass, brush, and forest communities; low to high elevations.

All Utah counties; AZ, CO, ID, MT, ND, NE, NM, NV, SD, WY.

Calochortus is derived from two Greek words meaning "beautiful grass." This can only be in reference to the flowers, since the few grass-like leaves are gone by blooming time. The first Utah pioneers ate significant quantities of Sego lilies to sustain themselves.

22

BRANDEGEE'S ONION
(*Allium brandegei*)
Lily Family (Liliaceae)

J F M A M J J A S O N D

Brandegee's Onion *is the shortest of the three wild onions described in this book. The tightly packed white flowers with a dark green stripe on the petals and sepals are beautiful. Like most onions, where you see one, you'll likely see many.*

 The flower cluster is an almost spherical umbel containing 5–35 flowers; each up to ½", white or occasionally pinkish, with a green stripe on each petal and sepal.

 Two flat, wide leaves per flower stalk, not shriveling up when the flowers bloom.

 Brush and forest communities; low to high elevations.

 Most Utah counties; western US.

 Brandegei is named for Townsend Brandegee (1843–1925) who developed an interest in botany while working as a civil engineer in NM. He collected plants in CA, NV, and Baja.

Up to 6"

23

PALMER'S ONION
(*Allium bisceptrum*)
Lily Family (Liliaceae)

JFMAMJJASOND

Onions can be a little difficult to tell apart; it requires an examination of the bulb. Short of digging up onions as you go, look for **Palmer's Onion** *to have a large cluster of pinkish flowers, each one having a 6-sided greenish crest in the center.*

Up to 16″

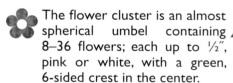

The flower cluster is an almost spherical umbel containing 8–36 flowers; each up to ½″, pink or white, with a green, 6-sided crest in the center.

2–4 flat, slender leaves, a little shorter than the flower stalk.

Brush and forest communities; low to high elevations.

Most Utah counties; AZ, NM, NV.

Other Names:
Aspen Onion

24

FALSE SOLOMON-SEAL
(*Smilacina racemosa*)
Lily Family (Liliaceae)

JFMAMJJASOND

False Solomon-seal *has long beautiful green leaves and a creamy white flower cluster that is gorgeous up close. Look for it in partially shaded spots in the late spring.*

 The flower cluster is up to 5″ long, with numerous small creamy white flowers.

 Mottled red, ¼″ berry; edible but bitter.

 5–10 per stem, up to 8″ long, lance shaped or oblong.

 Forest communities; low to high elevations.

 Most Utah counties; most of North America.

 Wild grouse enjoy the berries of False Solomon-seal.

Other Names:
Maianthemum racemosum

Up to 3′

25

ELEGANT DEATH CAMAS
(*Zigadenus elegans*)
Lily Family (Liliaceae)

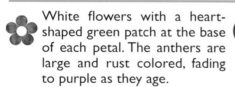

JFMAMJJASOND

Elegant Death Camas *has long, slender, grass-like leaves. The flower stalk rises above the leaves and has a loose cluster of intricate white and green flowers.*

Up to
2´

White flowers with a heart-shaped green patch at the base of each petal. The anthers are large and rust colored, fading to purple as they age.

Dark, glossy green basal leaves up to 12″ long and only ½″ wide.

Forest communities and alpine tundra; moderate to high elevations.

Most Utah counties; western North America.

Like the other Death Camas plants found in Utah, this one is poisonous. When the leaves first appear, it can be difficult to distinguish this plant from onions, and some of the other, nontoxic members of the Lily family.

Other Names:

Mountain Death Camas
Zigadenus glaucus
Anticlea chlorantha

JFMAMJJASOND

Look for **Foothills Death Camas** *in drier sites along the foothills above the benches. Leaves will appear first, followed by a large flower head rising on a central stalk. In bloom it is a fairly dense cone of white flowers with elements of yellow and gold.*

 White, ½" broad, 3 sepals and 3 petals, each with a yellowish patch at the base, large golden yellow anthers.

 Up to 16" long, narrow, concave and clasping; only found on the lower half of the flower stalk.

 Sagebrush and grass communities; low to moderate elevations.

 Most Utah counties; western US.

 Foothills Death Camas is even more poisonous than its cousin, Elegant Death Camas, on the previous page.

Other Names:

Toxicoscordion paniculatum

Helonias paniculatus

Up to 2 ½'

TUFTED EVENING-PRIMROSE
(*Oenothera caespitosa*)

Evening-primrose Family (Onagraceae)

JFMAMJJASOND

You need to be on the trail in the morning to see this low mound of beautiful, huge, white flowers. Better yet, find a **Tufted Evening-primrose** *in the evening and enjoy its wonderful fragrance.*

Up to 12″

 Pure white flowers, up to 4″ broad, very fragrant, closing up and turning pink after one evening; 4 heart-shaped petals, 4 pinkish sepals bent backward.

 Up to 6″ or more, slender, with a lot of variation in surface and edges, usually with a tuft of white hair along the leaf edges.

 Brush communities; low to moderate elevations.

 All Utah counties; western North America.

 Caespitosa means the plant has a tufted or clump-like growth habit.

WHITE BOG ORCHID
(*Habenaria dilatata*)
Orchid Family (Orchidaceae)

JFMAMJJASOND

White Bog Orchid, *with its tall spike of white flowers, is easy to spot. Look for it in moist, partially shady places. You'll often find Elephanthead nearby.*

 Cylindrical flower cluster up to 18″ long, each white flower about ⅓″.

 Up to 12″ long, lance shaped.

 Moist sites in canyon and meadow communities; low to high elevations.

 Most Utah counties; northern and western North America.

 Orchids are somewhat rare in Utah and should not be disturbed.

Other Names:
Platanthera leucostachys
Limnorchis leucostachys

Up to 4′

29

ARMED PRICKLY POPPY
(*Argemone munita*)
Poppy Family (Papaveraceae)

JFMAMJJASOND

Prickly Poppy *produces an abundance of gorgeous white blossoms on a tall, vicious looking plant. The large white petals are thin and wave in the slightest breeze. The center contains a mass of golden stamens surrounding a pistil with a reddish-purple stigma.*

Up to 4´

 White, up to 5˝ broad, 6 petals.

 Up to 6˝ long, lobed, spines on veins and usually between the veins.

 Desert brush, and Pinyon/Juniper communities; low to moderate elevations.

 Most Utah counties; AZ, CA, ID, NV, OR; Mexico.

Munita means "armed." With its spines and poisonous alkaloids, this plant is well armed indeed.

30

CARPET PHLOX
(*Phlox hoodii*)
Phlox Family (Polemoniaceae)

JFMAMJJASOND

Carpet Phlox *forms a low cushion, up to 12" across, of short, stiff, spiny leaves. In bloom the flowers can cover the whole plant. Pink or purplish flowers are also common. You may even see a plant with pink flowers growing next to one with white flowers.*

White, pinkish, or purplish, up to ¾" across with yellowish stamens.

Up to ½" long, needle shaped, with spiny tips, covered with shaggy white hair.

Desert brush and sagebrush communities; low to moderate elevations.

All Utah counties; western North America.

Hoodii is named after Robert Hood (d. 1821) who was a member of an ill-fated expedition to the Arctic, where he discovered Carpet Phlox.

Other Names:
Cushion Phlox
Spiny Phlox
Moss Phlox

Up to 4"

31

FLAXFLOWER
(*Linanthastrum nuttallii*)

Phlox Family (Polemoniaceae)

JFMAMJJASOND

Flaxflower *produces pretty little clumps of white flowers that show some yellow in the center from the stamens. Compare it to its Phlox cousin on the previous page.*

Up to 10″

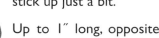 White, up to ½″ across, 5 petals, yellowish stamens that stick up just a bit.

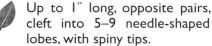 Up to 1″ long, opposite pairs, cleft into 5–9 needle-shaped lobes, with spiny tips.

 Forest communities; moderate to high elevations.

 Northern and central Wasatch Front; western US.

 Nuttallii is named for Thomas Nuttall (1786–1859) a curator of the Harvard Botanical Gardens, who traveled overland to Oregon in 1834. Flaxflower is not a true flax.

Other Names:

Nuttall's Linanthus
Linanthus nuttallii
Leptosiphon nuttallii

32

LEAFY JACOBSLADDER
(*Polemonium foliosissimum*)
Phlox Family (Polemoniaceae)

JFMAMJJASOND

Two varieties of Leafy Jacobsladder *overlap on the Wasatch Front. Alpinum, the variety with clusters of white blossoms, is very robust and quite common. Foliosissimum (variety name same as species name) has bluish-purple blossoms, and the plant is more delicate looking. Its range is from Utah county and southward.*

 Loose or tight globular clusters, creamy white or bluish-purple flowers, up to 1″ across.

 Up to 6″ long, 5–25 leaflets, lance shaped or elliptical, moderately to densely hairy.

 Aspen forest and grass communities; moderate to high elevations.

 Most Utah counties (between the two varieties); AZ, CO, ID, MT, NM, WY.

 Foliosissimum means "very leafy." Compare Leafy Jacobsladder to Pretty Jacobsladder in the purple flower section.

Up to 4′

33

LARGE COLLOMIA
(*Collomia grandiflora*)
Phlox Family (Polemoniaceae)

JFMAMJJASOND

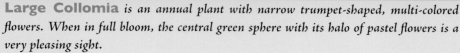

Large Collomia *is an annual plant with narrow trumpet-shaped, multi-colored flowers. When in full bloom, the central green sphere with its halo of pastel flowers is a very pleasing sight.*

Up to 20″

 About ½–1½″ long, trumpet shaped, showing pastel shades of pink, cream, or salmon. The sky-blue colored anthers add interest and contrast.

 Up to 2″ long, lance shaped, smooth edges, and alternating on the stem.

 Mountain brush and grass communities; low to moderate elevations.

 Most Utah counties; western North America.

 Collomia is from the Greek word *kolla*, meaning "glue," because of the sticky mucus on the seeds. *Grandiflora* means "large flower."

Second Species: Small Collomia (*Collomia linearis*), shown in the inset, has smaller flowers that are pink to purplish.

34

AMERICAN BISTORT
(*Polygonum bistortoides*)
Buckwheat Family (Polygonaceae)

J F M A M J J A S O N D

American Bistort *is very common in alpine meadows and creates a beautiful contrast, in both color and shape, to the other flowers in the meadow. It looks a bit like a giant Q-tip sticking up above the other plants.*

 Cylindrical cluster of numerous small white flowers, terminating a long stem, and having an offensive odor.

 Up to 8″ long, straight or oval, mostly basal.

 Moist meadows; moderate to high elevations.

 Most Utah counties; western North America.

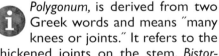 *Polygonum,* is derived from two Greek words and means "many knees or joints." It refers to the thickened joints on the stem. *Bistortoides* means "shaped like a Bistort." And *bistort* means "twice twisted," referring to the gnarled appearance of the dark brown rhizomes—which are eaten by bears and rodents. Deer and elk will eat the foliage.

Up to 2 ½″

Other Names:
Western Bistort
Smokeweed
Bistorta bistortoides

35

WHORLED BUCKWHEAT
(Eriogonum heracleoides)
Buckwheat Family (Polygonaceae)

JFMAMJJASOND

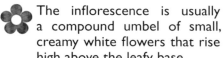

Whorled Buckwheat, *with its umbrella-like cluster of creamy white flowers, is easy to recognize because of the whorl of "leaves" (actually bracts) that are found about halfway up the stem (see picture inset).*

Up to 20″

The inflorescence is usually a compound umbel of small, creamy white flowers that rise high above the leafy base.

Up to 3″ long, elliptical or oblong, whitish with dense short hair on one or both surfaces, attached to a woody, mat-forming base.

Sagebrush and mountain brush communities; low to high elevations.

 Mountain counties in Utah; western North America, excluding AZ and NM.

 Heracleoides means "like the genus *Heracleum.*" Look at the Cow Parsnip on page 6 and you'll see a resemblance in the inflorescence.

Other Names:

Parsnipflower Buckwheat
Umbrella Plant

36

BANEBERRY
(*Actaea rubra*)
Buttercup Family (Ranunculaceae)

JFMAMJJASOND

Baneberry *is a beautiful, leafy plant that produces a large, rounded cone of white flowers. The flowers in turn produce shiny, fire-engine red, poisonous berries.*

 Cone-shaped cluster, up to 3″ long; numerous, ¼″, white flowers.

 Bright red berries up to ⅓″ long.

 Each leaf is divided once or twice in three leaflets; each leaflet up to 4″ long, usually with lobes and teeth.

 Forest communities; moderate to high elevations.

 All Utah; North America, excluding southeastern US.

 Rubra means "reddish."

Up to 3 ½′

37

MARSH MARIGOLD
(*Caltha leptosepala*)
Buttercup Family (Ranunculaceae)

JFMAMJJASOND

Marsh Marigold *is unique in appearance. It produces a single flower per stem with white petal-like sepals, numerous yellow stamens, and a center of five or more green pistils. Look for it in moist areas near the retreating snow line.*

Up to 20″

 Up to 2″ across, 5–12 white sepals, no petals, numerous yellow stamens, thick green pistils.

 Up to 4″ long, almost as broad, oval or heart shaped, dark glossy green with prominent veins.

 Wet meadows, stream banks, seeps; moderate to high elevations.

 Most Utah counties; western North America.

 Leptosepala means "narrow sepals."

Other Names:
White Marsh Marigold
Elkslip
Pyschrophila leptosepala

38

COLORADO COLUMBINE
(Aquilegia coerulea)
Buttercup Family (Ranunculaceae)

JFMAMJJASOND

The variety of **Colorado Columbine** *we have in Utah is usually a pure white, as shown above. Occasionally you'll come across one with some color (left inset), but you need to travel to Colorado to see why it's their state flower (right inset).*

 Pure white, sometimes with some purplish color, 2–3″ flowers, 5 petals with 3″ spurs, 5 perpendicular sepals; one or several flowers on each stem.

 Compound leaf up to 15″ long, usually divided twice into 3 leaflets.

 Mountain brush and forest communities; moderate to high elevations.

 All Utah counties; Rocky Mountain states.

 Coerulea comes from the Latin word for "blue."

Up to 4′

39

THIMBLEBERRY
(*Rubus parviflorus*)
Rose Family (Rosaceae)

JFMAMJJASOND

Thimbleberry *is a large, robust shrub with big, shiny leaves and large white flowers that later produce an edible, raspberry-like fruit.*

Up to 6′

 Loose clusters of several, 1½″, white flowers.

 Up to 6″ long and 8″ broad, maple-like lobes.

 Stream banks or moist areas in forest communities; low to moderate elevations.

 Most Utah counties; western North America and the Great Lakes region.

 Rubus is the Latin word for "bramble." The *Rubus* genus includes blackberries and raspberries.

Other Names:
Salmonberry

40

MALLOW-LEAVED NINEBARK
(Physocarpus malvaceus)
Rose Family (Rosaceae)

JFMAMJJASOND

If you hike any canyon trail in the Wasatch you'll likely spend some time brushing up against this large shrub. It has delicate green leaves with nice white flower clusters in the spring, becomes faded and torn by mid-summer, and finally turns a nice red in the fall.

 A hemispherical cluster, about 2″ in diameter, containing 5–30 white, fragrant flowers.

 About 1–3″ long and broad, divided into 3 main lobes, each lobe further divided into teeth or shallow lobes.

 Moist slopes and hillsides; low to moderate elevations.

 Most Utah counties; north-western North America.

 This species was named *Malvaceus* because the leaves resemble those of some of the Mallow family plants.

Up to 6′

41

SERVICEBERRY
(*Amelanchier alnifolia*)
Rose Family (Rosaceae)

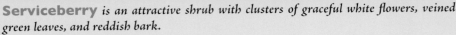

J F M A M J J A S O N D

Serviceberry *is an attractive shrub with clusters of graceful white flowers, veined green leaves, and reddish bark.*

Up to 15′

 White or sometimes pinkish flowers; five petals, ½″ or more long, 5 green sepals.

 1–2″, oval, serrated near the tip.

Streamsides, meadows, mountain slopes; low to high.

 Most Utah counties; western and northern North America.

 The whole plant is utilized as a food source for a large variety of wildlife.

Other Names:

Saskatoon

Shadbush

Second Species: Utah Serviceberry (*Amelanchier utahensis*) is a closely related species; with leaves less than 1″ long and petals only half the size of Serviceberry. (Not shown.)

42

CHOKECHERRY
(*Prunus virginiana*)
Rose Family (Rosaceae)

JFMAMJJASOND

This large shrub, or small tree, is a welcome addition to the canyons in the spring. **Chokecherry's** *glossy green leaves and numerous, large white flower clusters are very showy.*

 A dense, cylindrical cluster, 1–6″ long, of ½″ white blossoms.

 The fruit, which looks like a small cherry, is black when ripe, bitter tasting, and was used by the pioneers to make preserves.

 Elliptic and serrated, 1–4″ long.

 Sagebrush, Juniper, Oak communities; low to high elevations.

 All Utah counties; most of North America.

 Virginiana means "of, or from, Virginia." It's an important forage plant for wildlife, although new Chokecherry leaves are poisonous until the fruit ripens.

Up to 20–30′

43

SMALLFLOWER WOODLANDSTAR
(*Lithophragma parviflorum*)
Saxifrage Family (Saxifragaceae)

JFMAMJJASOND

Smallflower Woodlandstar *is a delicate beauty, appearing in mid-spring. The pure white petals, divided into lobes, and radiating from a small center, have a star-like appearance.*

Up to 18"

 Clusters of 4–7 white flowers; each flower up to ½", 5 deeply lobed petals.

 Up to 1½" long and 2" broad, divided into 3 lobes, each lobe again divided into smaller lobes.

 Sagebrush and forest communities; low to high elevations.

 Most Utah counties; western North America.

 Second Species: Fringecup (*Lithophragma glabrum*), shown on the right, is pink or white, and has reddish-purple bulblets in the flower cluster or leaf nodes.

Other Names:
Bulbous Woodlandstar
Lithophragma bulbiferum
   (for Fringecup)

44

FRINGED GRASS-OF-PARNASSUS
(Parnassia fimbriata)
Saxifrage Family (Saxifragaceae)

JFMAMJJASOND

What a delight to find this plant! The creamy white, fringed petals and intricate stamens make for a beautiful flower. Look for **Fringed Grass-of-Parnassus** *in moist areas.*

 Creamy white, up to 1½", 5 petals, fringed near the base.

 Up to 2" long and broad, basal only, heart shaped or kidney shaped.

Wet meadows, seeps and springs; low to high elevations.

 Most Utah counties; western North America.

 Parnassia is derived from Mt. Parnassus of Greece, but why that name was applied to this genus is unknown. *Fimbriata* means "fringed." Parnassus flowers are the symbol of clan MacLea in Scotland.

Up to 18"

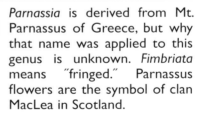

45

WESTERN VALERIAN
(*Valeriana occidentalis*)
Valerian Family (Valerianaceae)

JFMAMJJASOND

Western Valerian *has a distinctive appearance. The dense, rounded cluster of white flowers sits atop a long, thick stem containing just a few pairs of compound leaves.*

Up to 3′

Hemispherical cluster of numerous, ⅛″ white flowers.

Several opposite pairs of compound cauline leaves, separated by long lengths of stem; basal leaves up to 10″ long, usually with some side lobes.

Brush, forest, grass, alpine tundra communities; moderate to high elevations.

Most Utah counties; western US.

Related Species: There are two other Valerian species found on the Wasatch Front. Edible Valerian (*Valeriana edulis*), has a basal rosette of long, spatula-shaped leaves and an open and branching flower cluster. Mountain Valerian (*Valeriana acutiloba*) has larger, funnel-shaped flowers, and the cauline leaves are narrower and pointed.

HOUNDSTONGUE
(*Cynoglossum officinale*)
Borage Family (Boraginaceae)

JFMAMJJASOND

Houndstongue *is a leafy, weedy-looking plant that has been declared a noxious weed in certain States. The attractive bell-shaped flowers are predominantly a dark red and fade to a shade of purple or blue.*

 Each plant usually has many flower clusters. Each cluster has several bluish-red, 1/3" flowers.

 Up to 12" long, lance shaped, leafy to the top.

Sagebrush and forest communities; low to high elevations.

 Most Utah counties, all North America; native to Eurasia.

 Cynoglossum is derived from two Greek words and means "dog's tongue." Any plant with the species name *officinale* was originally considered to have medicinal qualities. However, Houndstongue is poisonous.

Other Names:

Gypsyflower

Up to 2′

47

HUMMINGBIRD FLOWER
(*Zauschneria latifolia*)
Evening-primrose Family (Onagraceae)

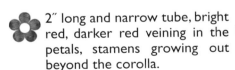

JFMAMJJASOND

As you hike in the canyons, you'll have to look up on the slopes or rock outcrops to see this plant. It grows in clumps, and the red flowers look a lot like chili peppers. When you see it, sit down for a while and listen for hummingbirds.

Up to 2'

 2" long and narrow tube, bright red, darker red veining in the petals, stamens growing out beyond the corolla.

Up to 2", lance shaped or elliptical, serrated.

 Rock outcrops, talus slopes; moderate to high elevations.

 Mountainous counties of Utah; AZ, CA, ID, NV, WY.

 Zauschneria is named for Johann Zauschner (1737–99), a professor of botany at Prague. This plant is pollinated by hummingbirds.

Other Names:
Epilobium canum

48

SCARLET GILIA
(Ipomopsis aggregata)
Phlox Family (Polemoniaceae)

JFMAMJJASOND

Scarlet Gilia *has eye-catching clusters of beautiful, trumpet-shaped, deep red flowers. Some populations have flowers that are a silvery white or pale pink. It is common and widespread in Utah.*

 In loose or dense clusters; each flower up to 2″ long, deep red, silvery white, or pinkish; the red flowers often have white speckles around the lobes.

 Up to 3″ long, finely divided into narrow leaflets, mostly basal, with a skunk-like odor.

 Wet or dry site in sagebrush and forest communities; low to moderate elevations.

 All Utah counties; western North America.

 Ipomopis, translates literally from Greek as "striking appearance." *Aggregata* means "clustered," referring to the shape of the inflorescence.

Other Names:

Polecat Plant

Gilia aggregata

 Up to 3′

49

COMMON PAINTBRUSH
(*Castilleja chromosa*)
Snapdragon Family (Scrophulariaceae)

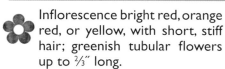

JFMAMJJASOND

Common Paintbrush *produces wonderfully deep splashes of red early in the season. Like all paintbrush species, the conspicuous colors are produced by the bracts that surround the greenish tubular flowers.*

Up to 2′

Inflorescence bright red, orange red, or yellow, with short, stiff hair; greenish tubular flowers up to ⅔″ long.

Covered with short, stiff hair; lower leaves are narrowly lance shaped, upper leaves usually divided into 3 narrow lobes.

Desert brush, sagebrush, and Pinyon/Juniper communities; low to high elevations.

All Utah counties; western US.

Second Species: Wavy-leaf Paintbrush (*Castilleja applegatei*), shown in the inset, has wavy leaf edges and glands that make it sticky or tacky. It blooms later in the season, and in Utah is found at higher elevations in the Wasatch and Uintah mountains.

Other Names
Castilleja angustifolia

50

RHEXIA-LEAF PAINTBRUSH

(Castilleja rhexiifolia)

Snapdragon Family (Scrophulariaceae)

JFMAMJJASOND

Rhexia-leaf Paintbrush *is common in the mountain meadows and produces a variety colors. The green tubular flower is long and conspicuous, and is surrounded by a dense arrangement of colored bracts that often curl a bit at their edges.*

 Inflorescence bright red, pink, or whitish-yellow, with short hair; greenish tubular flowers, up to 1½″ long.

 Up to 3″ long, broadly lance shaped, prominent veins, occasionally with short hair.

 Moist alpine meadows and slopes; high elevations.

 Most Utah counties; western US and Canada.

 Rhexiifolia means "having leaves like *Rhexia*," which is a genus in the Meadow-beauty family and is not found in Utah.

Other Names:

Split-leaf Paintbrush

Castilleja sulphurea
   (for the yellow variety)

Up to 15″

51

EATON'S PENSTEMON
(*Penstemon eatonii*)
Snapdragon Family (Scrophulariaceae)

JFMAMJJASOND

Driving through the canyons, your eye will constantly be drawn to **Eaton's Penstemon** *growing on the canyon wall with the bright red, tubular flowers that jut out from one side of the stem. Each patch will seem more beautiful than the last.*

Up to 4′

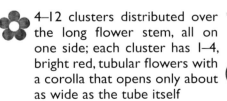
4–12 clusters distributed over the long flower stem, all on one side; each cluster has 1–4, bright red, tubular flowers with a corolla that opens only about as wide as the tube itself

Up to 8″ long, oval or broadly lance shaped, usually with wavy edges.

Numerous habitats, often on talus slopes; low to high elevations.

Most Utah counties; AZ, CA, CO, ID, NM, NV, WY.

Eatonii is named for Daniel Eaton (1834–85), a professor of botany and an herbarium curator at Yale University who traveled to Utah in the 1860s.

Other Names:
Firecracker Penstemon

SHOWY MILKWEED
(Asclepias speciosa)
Milkweed Family (Asclepiadaceae)

JFMAMJJASOND

Showy Milkweed *is a very stout, robust plant with large leaves and a truly incredible cluster of beautiful and intricate flowers.*

 Very large globular cluster; flowers intricate, in shades of reddish-pink, pink, and white.

 A 3″ seedpod (right inset) containing many brown seeds attached to a dandelion-like silky parachute.

 Up to 2″ long, broadly lance shaped, thick midvein.

Moist sites, fields, roadsides; low to moderate elevations.

 Most Utah counties; central and western North America.

Asclepias is derived from the word for the Greek god of medicine, and milkweeds were anciently used in medicines. However, they are poisonous to cattle and horses. Like Flax, it has long fibers that were used by Native Americans to make cordage.

Up to 3 ½′

53

UTAH THISTLE
(*Cirsium neomexicanum*)
Sunflower Family (Asteraceae)

JFMAMJJASOND

Utah Thistle *is tall and stout with a thick stem and numerous, large, regularly lobed leaves. Both are covered with short hair, giving it a grayish appearance. The flower head is large and produces numerous pale pink disk flowers.*

Up to 3′

 Pink to white, disk flowers only; spiny flower head, up to 1″ tall and 2″ wide, with some long white hair on the spiny bracts.

 Deeply lobed basal leaf, up to 10″ long, lobes again divided into lobes, spiny, covered with short white hair; cauline leaves gradually becoming smaller.

 Desert brush, sagebrush, Pinyon/Juniper communities; low to moderate elevations.

 Wasatch Front; AZ, NM, NV.

 There are two varieties of this species in Utah. This variety, Utah Thistle, is found primarily on the Wasatch Front. The other variety, New Mexico Thistle can be found in central and southern Utah and usually presents with creamy white flowers.

NODDING THISTLE
(*Carduus nutans*)
Sunflower Family (Asteraceae)

JFMAMJJASOND

Nodding Thistle *is beautiful in bud and flower. The reddish-pink color is very intense! In early summer you'll see lots of it on the roadsides and in empty lots and fields.*

 Brilliant reddish-pink flower up to 3″ across, usually one per stalk, with numerous broad, spine-tipped bracts.

 Up to 16″ long, shiny green, lobed, and with spines.

 Roadsides and disturbed sites in mountain brush and sagebrush communities; low to moderate elevations.

 All Utah counties; all US.

 Carduus is the old Latin name for thistles. *Nutans* means "nodding or drooping." This plant is a native of Europe and started spreading throughout Utah in the 1960s.

Other Names:

Musk Thistle

Up to 7′

55

ROCKY MOUNTAIN BEEPLANT
(*Cleome serrulata*)
Caper Family (Capparaceae)

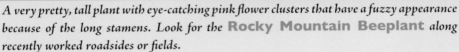

JFMAMJJASOND

A very pretty, tall plant with eye-catching pink flower clusters that have a fuzzy appearance because of the long stamens. Look for the **Rocky Mountain Beeplant** *along recently worked roadsides or fields.*

Up to 6′

 Cylindrical cluster of numerous pink flowers with stamens extending well beyond the flower corolla.

 Long, slender pods; up to 4″.

 Up to 3″, lance shaped, 3 leaflets per leaf.

A pioneer plant of disturbed sites; low to moderate elevations.

 All Utah counties; North America, excluding southeastern US.

 Cleome was the ancient name for some mustard-like plants. Native Americans ate the leaves and flowers of beeplant.

56

MOUNTAIN SNOWBERRY
(*Symphoricarpos oreophilus*)
Honeysuckle Family (Caprifoliaceae)

JFMAMJJASOND

Mountain Snowberry *has oval green leaves and scattered clusters of pink tubular flowers. It is common on the Wasatch Front. But if you don't catch it in bloom, look again in the late summer for the large white berries.*

 One to several flowers per cluster; pink, ½″ long, tubular.

 White, poisonous berries; ¼–½″ across, slightly longer.

 Up to 2″ long, elliptical or oval, prominent veins.

 Sagebrush and forest communities; moderate to high elevations.

 Most Utah counties; western North America.

Up to 4′

 Symphoricarpos is derived from two Greek words meaning "borne together" and "fruit," in reference to the clusters of berries. *Oreophilus* means "mountain loving."

Other Names:

Symphoricarpos utahensis

Symphoricarpos rotundifolius

57

UTAH SWEETPEA
(*Lathyrus pauciflorus*)
Pea Family (Fabaceae)

JFMAMJJASOND

Utah Sweetpea *climbs over other plants around it and usually only has one or two flower clusters. The beautiful, multi-colored flowers have a faint sweet smell.*

Up to 4′

 Clusters of 3–8 flowers; each flower up to 1″ long, bi- or tri-colored, banner pink or purple, wings and keel pale pink or white.

 Leaf stem up to 5″ long, with 8–12, 1½″ oval or elliptical leaflets alternating on the stem.

 Mountain brush, meadow, and forest communities; low to high elevations.

Northern Utah counties; CA, CO, ID, OR.

 There are several species of Sweetpea in Utah not shown here. If the plant has some hair sticking out from the stems and leaves, it's probably Rydberg's Sweetpea (*Lathyrus brachycalyx*). If the banner is cream or pale pink with dark pinkish-red veins, it's probably Lanszwert's Sweetpea (*Lathyrus lanszwertii*).

AMERICAN VETCH
(*Vicia americana*)
Pea Family (Fabaceae)

American Vetch *uses coil-like tendrils to cling to other nearby plants. Its pinkish or purplish flowers strongly resemble the flowers of the Sweet Pea. Although you have to dissect the flower to tell the difference, in general American Vetch blooms later, has narrower and more numerous leaflets, and does not have multicolored flowers.*

 Clusters of 3–10 flowers; up to 1″ long, purplish-pink, pea-like flower, aging to a bluish color.

 Leaf stem up to 8″ long with an even number (8–16) of 1½″ leaflets.

 Mountain brush and forest communities; low to high elevations.

 All Utah counties; most of North America.

 Fava beans, which have been part of the Mediterranean diet since around 6000 BC, are part of this same genus.

Up to 4″

59

NORTHERN SWEETVETCH
(*Hedysarum boreale*)
Pea Family (Fabaceae)

JFMAMJJASOND

Northern Sweetvetch *is similar to American Vetch on the previous page, but grows more like a bush and has larger, denser flower clusters. The flowers tend to be on the reddish side of pink, and the keel is longer than the wings and blunt on the end.*

Up to 2 ½'

 Spike-shaped clusters of 5–45 flowers; up to 1″ long, reddish-pink, pea-like flower; keel blunt, extending beyond the wings.

 Flattened pods, constricted between the seeds, appearing like a short segment of a motorcycle chain.

 Compound leaf up to 5″ long; 5–15 leaflets, up to 1½″ long, arranged in two parallel rows.

 Desert shrub, mountain brush and forest communities; low to high elevations.

 Most Utah counties; western US; all Canada.

 Northern Sweetvetch is edible, with roots that taste like licorice, and it was eaten by Native Americans. However, it resembles some of the poisonous Milkvetch (*Astragalus*) species, so you should avoid doing a taste test.

60

UTAH MILKVETCH
(Astragalus utahensis)

Pea Family (Fabaceae)

JFMAMJJASOND

Utah Milkvetch *forms mats on roadcuts and all over the benches and terraces of the old Bonneville shoreline in the spring. Its magnificently colored flowers are striking against the hairy gray leaves.*

 Clusters of 2–12 flowers; each flower up to 1″ long, purplish-pink, pea-like, with a white stripe in the center of the banner.

 The seed pods are covered with long white hair, giving them the appearance of a small cotton ball.

 Leaf stem up to 4″ long, with an odd number (9–19) of 1″ leaflets covered with short white hair.

 Brush and Pinyon/Juniper communities; low to moderate elevations.

 All except the eastern Utah counties; ID, NV.

 The Milkvetch plants are also known as Locoweeds. Many of them contain poisonous alkaloids, and some of them can take up selenium from the soil, which is also poisonous.

Up to 5″

61

BROWSE MILKVETCH
(*Astragalus cibarius*)
Pea Family (Fabaceae)

JFMAMJJASOND

As with Utah Milkvetch on the previous page, Browse Milkvetch *is common in the foothills of the Wasatch Front. The combination of white wings, purplish-pink keel, and pink and white banner is striking!*

Up to 12"

 Clusters of 4–14 flowers; each flower up to ⅔" long, purplish-pink, with white wings.

 Compound leaf up to 4" long, with an odd number (11–19) of ½" leaflets, smooth on the upper surface, hairy on the underside.

 Desert shrub, brush and Pinyon/Juniper communities; low to high elevations.

 Most Utah counties; CO, ID, MT, NV, WY.

i *Astragalus* is derived from the Greek word for "ankle bone" and refers to the shape of the seeds of some species.

62

STICKY GERANIUM
(*Geranium viscosissimum*)
Geranium Family (Geraniaceae)

J F M A M J J A S O N D

Sticky Geranium *is one of the first flowers we learn to identify; it's pretty, grows in so many habitats, and blooms somewhere all summer. Don't ignore the leaves and stems, which are, large, showy, and turn nice red colors as fall approaches.*

 About 1″, pale pink to deep pink flowers, with darker pink insect guidelines; one or several flowers per stalk.

 Up to 3″ long and 6″ broad; divided into 5–7 large lobes, each divided into smaller lobes.

 Sagebrush, mountain brush, forest communities; low to high elevations.

 Most Utah counties; western North America

 Viscosissimum means "very sticky," although the Wasatch Front plants seem only mildly so. It's an important forage plant for wild animals.

Up to 4′

TAPERTIP ONION
(*Allium acuminatum*)
Lily Family (Liliaceae)

JFMAMJJASOND

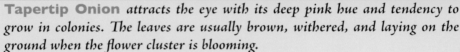

Tapertip Onion *attracts the eye with its deep pink hue and tendency to grow in colonies. The leaves are usually brown, withered, and laying on the ground when the flower cluster is blooming.*

Up to 12″

 The flower cluster is a hemispherical umbel containing 15–40 flowers; each up to ½″, purplish-pink or rose pink, tapering to a point, bent backward.

 2–4 curved (not flat), slender leaves, a little shorter than the flower stalk.

 Brush and forest communities; low to moderate elevations.

Most Utah counties; western North America.

 Acuminatum refers to the tapering point of the petals and sepals. The bulbs are edible, but small and deeply buried. Compare with Palmer's and Brandegee's Onion in the white flower section.

WILD HOLLYHOCK
(Iliamna rivularis)
Mallow Family (Malvaceae)

JFMAMJJASOND

Wild Hollyhock *is not huge like the domestic hollyhocks, but equally as beautiful. The pink buds and flowers and broad maple-like leaves are very attractive.*

 About 2″ broad, rose pink to pale pink flowers.

 Up to 6″ long and broad; divided into 3–7 triangular, serrated lobes.

 Streams and moist sites; low to high elevations.

 Most Utah counties; northwestern US, southwestern Canada.

 Rivularis means "growing by streams." Wild Hollyhock is one of the first species to appear after a fire.

Up to 5′

Other Names:
Mountain Globemallow
Mountain Hollyhock
Maple Mallow

OREGON CHECKER
(*Sidalcea oregana*)
Mallow Family (Malvaceae)

Oregon Checker *has beautiful pink flowers very similar to Wild Hollyhock on the previous page. Look at the leaves to distinguish them. Oregon Checker's leaves are not maple-like, and the lobes of the upper leaves become deeper and narrower.*

Up to 4′

 About 2″ broad, rose pink to pale pink flowers.

 Basal leaves up to 6″ long and broad, divided into 5–7 shallow lobes; cauline leaves deeply cut into long, narrow lobes.

 Stream banks, meadows, open forest; low to moderate elevations.

 Wasatch Front; western US, excluding AZ, CO, NM.

 Sidalcea is derived from two different Greek words for the Mallow family. *Oregana* means "of Oregon."

66

FIREWEED
(Epilobium angustifolium)
Evening-primrose Family (Onagraceae)

JFMAMJJASOND

Fireweed is on everyone's top ten list. It's a very pretty, tall plant with eye-catching pink/maroon flower clusters and long, narrow, pointed leaves.

 Cylindrical cluster containing buds, flowers, and seed pods simultaneously; 1½" flowers with 4 pink petals and 4 narrow, maroon sepals.

 Up to 8", lance shaped.

 Mountain brush and forest communities; moderate to high elevations.

 All Utah counties; most of North America.

 Epilobium is derived from two Greek words meaning "upon a pod," which refers to how the flower forms at the tip of the seed pod. *Angustifolium* means "narrow leaved." Fireweed's common name is due to the fact that it is one of the first plants to colonize after a fire.

Other Names:
Chamerion angustifolium

Up to 7'

67

BROAD-LEAVED CLARKIA
(*Clarkia rhomboidea*)
Evening-primrose Family (Onagraceae)

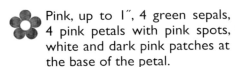
JFMAMJJASOND

Broad-leaved Clarkia *is a short plant that can be found hiding under the scrub oak along trails in the foothills. Its beautifully marked pink flower bears a strong resemblance to its more showy cousin, Fireweed, on the previous page.*

Up to 20″

 Pink, up to 1″, 4 green sepals, 4 pink petals with pink spots, white and dark pink patches at the base of the petal.

 Up to 2″, oval or elliptical with pointed ends.

 Mountain brush communities; low to moderate elevations.

Wasatch Front; states west of and including MT, UT, AZ.

 Clarkia, is named for William Clark (1770–1838) of Lewis and Clark fame. *Rhomboidea* means ″diamond shaped″ in reference to the shape of the petals.

Other Names:
Diamond Clarkia

LONGLEAF PHLOX
(Phlox longifolia)
Phlox Family (Polemoniaceae)

JFMAMJJASOND

Longleaf Phlox *is a short plant with multiple stems that have several pink to pale lavender blossoms. The flowers have five pink lobes, fading to white near the center, with gold colored stamens peeking out. The flower head appears striped.*

 Pink, white, or lavender, up to 1″ across, gold stamens; calyx of 5 sepals, each with a dark ridge, giving the calyx a striped appearance.

 Up to 3″ long, narrow, covered with sticky hair.

 Desert brush, sagebrush, and forest communities; low to high elevations.

 All Utah counties; western North America.

 Longifolia is Latin for "long leaf." It's one of the earliest spring flowers and blooms well into summer.

Up to 16″

69

ALPINE COLLOMIA
(*Collomiastrum debile*)
Phlox Family (Polemoniaceae)

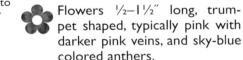
JFMAMJJASOND

This exceptionally beautiful plant is usually found growing on dry, barren-looking talus slopes. **Alpine Collomia** *forms a compact mound and is covered with gorgeous pink flowers when in bloom.*

Up to 6″

Flowers ½–1½″ long, trumpet shaped, typically pink with darker pink veins, and sky-blue colored anthers.

Up to 2″, reverse lance shaped, covered with sticky hairs.

A high-elevation plant, usually found on talus slopes.

 Juab, Salt Lake, Utah, and Wasatch counties; most western states of the United States.

 Debile means weak or frail, and refers to the stems, which lay flat instead of standing up. In high-elevation climates with mountain winds, this is actually an advantage.

Other Names:
Collomia debilis

70

JFMAMJJASOND

Springbeauty *blooms in synchrony with the movement of spring up the mountain slopes. Keep your eyes looking low to the ground, and you should be able to spot its pink to white blooms with darker pink veins.*

 Pink to white, up to 1"; 5 petals, darker pink veins, yellow patches at the base.

 Up to 4" long, oval, oblong, or lance shaped, thick, usually two per stem.

 Mountain brush and forest communities; low to high elevations.

 Most Utah counties; western US.

Up to 8"

 Claytonia, is named for John Clayton (d. 1770) one of the earliest collectors of plant specimens in Virginia. *Lanceolata* means "lance-like" and refers to the shape of the leaves. The stems arise from a corm that is edible.

71

PARRY'S PRIMROSE
(*Primula parryi*)
Primrose Family (Primulaceae)

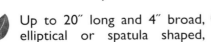

JFMAMJJASOND

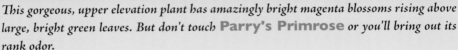

This gorgeous, upper elevation plant has amazingly bright magenta blossoms rising above large, bright green leaves. But don't touch **Parry's Primrose** *or you'll bring out its rank odor.*

Up to 20″

Arranged in umbels of 3–20, magenta, 1″ flowers; each having 5 lobes and a yellow center.

Up to 20″ long and 4″ broad, elliptical or spatula shaped, basal leaves only.

Meadows, talus slopes, stream banks; high elevations.

 Most Utah counties; AZ, CO, ID, MT, NM, NV, WY.

 Parryi is named for Dr. Charles Parry (1823–90), an explorer and naturalist who discovered many new species in the southwestern US.

72

JFMAMJJASOND

Pretty Shooting Star *can be hard to spot because it's often surrounded by grasses and plants. If you find a spot of spongy ground, examine it carefully and you may find a Shooting Star.*

 Up to 1″ long, lavender to magenta, white and yellow rings at the corolla base; stamens fused together into a yellow and black tube.

 Up to 12″, narrowly elliptical.

 Springs, seeps, moist sites in meadows; low to high elevations.

 All Utah counties; western North America.

Second Species: Alpine Shooting Star (*Dodecatheon alpinum*), shown in the inset, is shorter, has only 4 of the bent back corolla lobes, and is not as widely distributed.

Up to 2′

VIOLET BUTTERCUP
(*Ranunculus andersonii*)
Buttercup Family (Ranunculaceae)

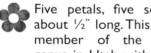

The **Buttercup** *family includes many beautiful plants, but this is one of the most distinctive and exciting to find. Hike the trail on the west side of Stansbury Island in mid-March and you're likely see it.*

Up to 8″

Five petals, five sepals, both about ½″ long. This is the only member of the *Ranunculus* genus in Utah with reddish or purplish petals and sepals.

Up to about 3″ long, each leaf divided several times into 3 leaflets.

Hillsides in desert brush communities.

Western counties of Utah; AZ, CA, NV.

Andersonii is named after Dr. Charles Lewis Anderson, a physician and naturalist who collected plants in Nevada during the 1860s.

Other Names:
Anderson's Buttercup

74

NOOTKA ROSE
(*Rosa nutkana*)
Rose Family (Rosaceae)

JFMAMJJASOND

Nootka Rose *is deliciously fragrant! It has five deep pink petals and a nicely contrasting mass of bright yellow stamens. Look for it blooming along the trails in late spring.*

 Pink, with 5 petals and sepals, each up to 1½″ long, numerous bright yellow stamens, very fragrant.

 Known as "hips," globular, up to ¾″ across, red to purplish.

 Compound leaf, up to 5″ long, with 5–7 serrated leaflets.

 Brush and forest communities; low to high elevations.

 Most Utah counties; western US.

Second Species: Another Rose species, Woods' Rose (*Rosa woodsii*), is commonly found on the Wasatch Front. It has smaller sepals, petals, and fruit. Also, where Nootka Rose tends to have a solitary flower on each stem, Woods' Rose tends to have two or more.

Up to 6′

75

RED ALUMROOT
(*Heuchera rubescens*)
Saxifrage Family (Saxifragaceae)

JFMAMJJASOND

Look in the cracks of nearly vertical rock faces to find this pretty plant with healthy green leaves and graceful red stems with a loose grouping of pink-white flowers.

Up to 12″

 Inflorescence is up to 7″ long; each flower ¼″ long, pink sepals and white petals.

 Up to 2″ wide and broad, shallow lobes or teeth, spring-green in color, thick.

 Rock outcroppings; moderate to high elevations.

 Central and northern Utah counties; western US.

 *Heuchera* is named for Johann Heinrich von Heucher (1677–1747), a professor at Wittenberg Germany. *Rubescens* mean reddish or to become red.

Other Names:
Wild Coralbells
Mountain Alumroot
Pink Alumroot

ELEPHANTHEAD
(*Pedicularis groenlandica*)
Snapdragon Family (Scrophulariaceae)

JFMAMJJASOND

Elephanthead *is first seen as a long purplish-pink spike among the grasses and sedges of wet areas. Up close, the individual flowers bear a marvelous resemblance to an elephant's head and trunk.*

 Dense cylindrical cluster; purplish-pink, ½″ flowers, resembling the head and trunk of an elephant.

 Up to 10″ long, fern-like, composed of parallel rows of narrow leaflets.

 Wet sites in forest, alpine tundra, and sedge/grass communities; moderate to high elevations.

 Most Utah counties; western US, Canada.

 Pedicularis is derived from the Latin word for "louse." It was once believed that cattle eating plants of this genus would have more lice. Elephanthead is a parasite on the roots of grasses and sedges.

Other Names:
Elephanthead Lousewort

Up to 28″

77

LEWIS' MONKEYFLOWER
(*Mimulus lewisii*)
Snapdragon Family (Scrophulariaceae)

J F M A M J J A S O N D

Wow! The shape, colors, spots, and hair of this exceptionally beautiful flower belong in a tropical rainforest!

Up to 3′

 Up to 2″ long; pink, red, or magenta; yellow on the lower throat with red spots and straight, stiff hair.

 Up to 3″ long, oval to lance shaped, in pairs on the stem, with prominent veins.

 Wet areas, stream banks; moderate to high elevations.

 Northern Wasatch Front; western North America, excluding AZ, NM.

 Lewisii is named after Meriweather Lewis, who found this plant near Glacier National Park.

Other Names:
Purple Monkeyflower

78

PALMER'S PENSTEMON
(Penstemon palmeri)
Snapdragon Family (Scrophulariaceae)

JFMAMJJASOND

The height of this plant and its large number of flowering stems and big pink flowers attract a lot of attention. The flowers are beautiful and have a pleasing scent.

 4–20 clusters distributed over the tall flower stem; each cluster has 1–5 creamy pink, fragrant, bulbous flowers with reddish-pink insect guidelines and tufts of golden hair.

 Up to 5″ long, often with a whitish coating, lance shaped and completely surrounding the stem.

 Desert shrub, mountain brush, and forest communities; low to high elevations.

 Most Utah counties; AZ, CA, CO, ID, NM, NV, WA, WY.

 Palmeri is named for Edward Palmer (1830–1911), an Englishman and self-taught botanist, who collected over 100,000 botanical specimens. This plant's range has been greatly extended in Utah by its inclusion in seed mixtures and its use in reclamation plantings.

Other Names:
Scented Penstemon

 Up to 5′

79

ORANGE AGOSERIS
(*Agoseris aurantiaca*)
Sunflower Family (Asteraceae)

JFMAMJJASOND

This easily recognizable flower is one of the few orange wildflowers and it looks very much like an orange dandelion.

Up to 20″

1″ brownish-orange flower; ray flowers only, no disk; each petal squared off and with 5 teeth.

Only basal leaves, up to 15″ long, over 1″ broad, and sometimes toothed or lobed.

Sagebrush, mountain brush, and alpine meadow communities; moderate to high elevations.

Most Utah counties; western North America.

Agoseris is the Greek name for "goat chicory." *Aurantiaca* means "orange-red." Like dandelions, the greens and flowers are edible.

Other Names:

Orange Mountain Dandelion

COMMON GLOBEMALLOW
(*Sphaeralcea coccinea*)
Mallow Family (Malvaceae)

JFMAMJJASOND

Common Globemallow *often grows in colonies. In the spring of a good year it stains the hillsides and desert valleys with patches of rusty orange.*

 Up to 1½", with 5 reddish-orange, heart-shaped petals.

 Up to 2" broad, 1½" long, divided into 3–5 finger-like lobes, each lobe also with teeth or lobes.

 Desert brush and mountain brush communities; low to moderate elevations.

 All Utah counties; western North America.

 Coccinea means "scarlet." There are 14 Globemallows in Utah and they can be difficult to distinguish. Common Globemallow, is just that, the most common and widely distributed in the state.

Other Names:
Scarlet Globemallow
Scarlet Falsemallow

Up to 12"

81

ARROWLEAF BALSAMROOT
(*Balsamorhiza sagittata*)
Sunflower Family (Asteraceae)

JFMAMJJASOND

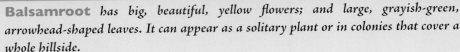

Balsamroot *has big, beautiful, yellow flowers; and large, grayish-green, arrowhead-shaped leaves. It can appear as a solitary plant or in colonies that cover a whole hillside.*

Up to 3′

 Yellow, up to 4″ across, with the underside covered with cobwebby hair

 Up to 18″ long and 6″ broad, shaped like an arrowhead and with a thick coating of short hair.

 Hillsides; low to moderate elevations.

 Most Utah counties; western North America.

 There are three other Balsamroot species in Utah, but this is the most common. Grazing animals enjoy it. Its height, color, and tendency to cover a hillside can cause it to be confused with Mulesears and true sunflowers. A brief examination of the leaves will distinguish it.

82

MULESEARS
(*Wyethia amplexicaulis*)
Sunflower Family (Asteraceae)

JFMAMJJASOND

Mulesears *has big, beautiful yellow flowers and large, shiny green leaves, angled almost vertically. It usually appears in colonies on a hillside.*

 Yellow, up to 3½″ across, with wide, shiny flower heads.

 Up to 16″ long and 6″ broad, and shiny as if varnished; the cauline leaves are smaller, pointed, and clasp the stem.

 Sagebrush, open forest, and grass communities; low to high elevations.

 North and central Utah counties; northwestern US.

 Wyethia is named for Nathaniel Wyeth (1802–56), a fur trader who established Fort Hall, near Pocatello, Idaho. *Amplexicaulis* refers to how the upper leaves clasp the stem.

Up to 3′

83

COMMON SUNFLOWER
(*Helianthus annuus*)
Sunflower Family (Asteraceae)

JFMAMJJASOND

Common Sunflower *is a tall, rough plant with large yellow ray flowers and dark brown disk flowers. You'll find lots of it on the roadsides in late summer.*

Up to 13′

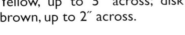 Yellow, up to 5″ across; disk brown, up to 2″ across.

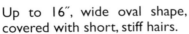 Up to 16″, wide oval shape, covered with short, stiff hairs.

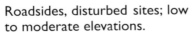 Roadsides, disturbed sites; low to moderate elevations.

 All Utah counties; all North America.

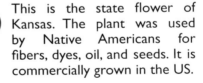 This is the state flower of Kansas. The plant was used by Native Americans for fibers, dyes, oil, and seeds. It is commercially grown in the US.

ONEHEAD SUNFLOWER
(Helianthella uniflora)
Sunflower Family (Asteraceae)

JFMAMJJASOND

Onehead Sunflower *is often seen growing in clumps. It has lots of green leaves and each stem usually has a single, large yellow flower.*

 Yellow, up to 5″ across; disk a darker yellow.

 Up to 6″, lance shaped or elliptical, with three prominent veins.

 Brush and forest communities; low to high elevations.

 Most Utah counties; CO, ID, MT, NM, NV, OR, WY.

Helianthella means "little sunflower." It looks similar to Showy Goldeneye on the next page, but has rougher stems and leaves and finishes blooming about the time that Goldeneye starts to appear. It is a common food source for grazing animals.

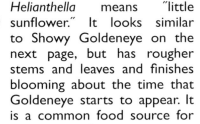

Up to 3′

85

SHOWY GOLDENEYE
(*Viguiera multiflora*)
Sunflower Family (Asteraceae)

JFMAMJJASOND

Showy Goldeneye *looks like a small yellow sunflower with a dark gold center. If you hike a trail at the end of August, you may pass thousands of them.*

Up to 3 ½'

 Yellow, up to 1 ½" across, disk a darker yellow than the rays.

Up to 3", lance shaped, veined, usually a dark green.

Sagebrush and forest communities; low to high elevations.

 All Utah counties; western US.

 Viguiera is named for Louis Viguier (1790–1867), a French botanist. *Multiflora* means "many flowered."

Other Names:

Heliomeris multiflora

86

HEARTLEAF ARNICA
(*Arnica cordifolia*)
Sunflower Family (Asteraceae)

JFMAMJJASOND

Heartleaf Arnica *has a big yellow flower, and lower leaves that are usually heart shaped. It is one of the first yellow daisy-like flowers of the season. Look for it in partial shade at the edges of the forest.*

 Yellow, up to 3″ across; usually one per stem.

 Lower leaves are heart shaped, up to 3½″ long and broad, serrated; upper leaves are lance shaped and attached directly to the stem.

 Forest communities; low to high elevations.

 Most Utah counties; western North America.

 Cordifolia means "heart-shaped leaves." There are three other Arnicas that share the same range and general appearance as Heartleaf Arnica. You need to carefully examine the leaves and tear apart the flower heads to distinguish them. They are: Hairy Arnica (*Arnica mollis*), Broadleaf Arnica (*Arnica latifolia*), and Varying Arnica (*Arnica diversifolia*). The flowers of a related species of Arnica (*Arnica montana*) are used to create a topical medication.

Up to 16″

87

GAUGE PLANT
(*Senecio integerrimus*)
Sunflower Family (Asteraceae)

JFMAMJJASOND

Gauge Plant *is one of the first yellow, daisy-like flowers to appear in spring. Look for a cluster of about a dozen flowers at the top of a slender stem, often with cobwebby hair on the flower head and stem.*

Up to 2′

 Flat-topped cluster of yellow flowers; each flower up to 1″ across, often with cobwebby hair on the flower head.

 Up to 5″ long, variously shaped, mostly basal leaves, the few stems leaves are smaller.

 Brush and forest communities; low to high elevations.

 All Utah counties; western North America.

 Senecio is derived from the Latin word for "old man," perhaps referring to the numerous white bristles attached to the seeds. Ranchers have used the appearance of this flower to "gauge" when a range was ready for grazing.

Other Names:

Lambstongue Ragwort
Single-stem Groundsel

UINTA GROUNDSEL
(Senecio multilobatus)
Sunflower Family (Asteraceae)

JFMAMJJASOND

Uinta Groundsel *is common throughout the Wasatch Front. It's a cheerful plant with dense clusters of small yellow flowers and leaves that are lobed (see inset).*

 Flat-topped cluster of yellow flowers; each flower up to ¾″ across.

 Up to 5″ long, deeply lobed, toothed, mostly basal leaves, the few stem leaves are smaller.

 Desert shrub, brush, and forest communities; low to high elevations.

 All Utah counties; most of western US.

 Multilobatus means "many lobed." In the Wasatch Mountains there is an almost identical species, Manyface Groundsel (*Senecio streptanthifolius*), which has basal leaves that are not lobed.

Other Names:
Basin Butterweed
Lobeleaf Groundsel
Packera multilobata

Up to 2′

89

DESERT GROUNDSEL
(*Senecio eremophilus*)
Sunflower Family (Asteraceae)

JFMAMJJASOND

Desert Groundsel's *leggy appearance, lobed leaves, and black tips on the bracts of the flower head make it easy to recognize.*

Up to 3′

Bright yellow, several to many in a cluster, up to 1″ across, black tips on the bracts.

Up to 6″ long, lobed in parallel rows.

Grass, forest, and alpine tundra communities; low to high elevations.

Wasatch Front and Uintahs; western North America.

Eremophilus means "desert loving," although Desert Groundsel can be found from the high desert valleys up to the alpine tundra.

Other Names:
Desert Ragwort

90

FREMONT'S GROUNDSEL
(Senecio fremontii)
Sunflower Family (Asteraceae)

JFMAMJJASOND

Fremont's Groundsel typically appears as a mounded shape of thick, serrated leaves topped with moderately large, bright yellow flowers. Look for it on rocky hillsides at high elevations.

 Bright yellow, several in a cluster, up to 1″ across, flower head somewhat bulbous with purplish tips.

 Up to 3″ long, oval, tapering at the base, often somewhat serrated.

 Spruce/Pine and alpine tundra communities; high elevations.

 Wasatch Front and Uintahs; western North America.

 Fremontii is named for John Charles Fremont (1813–90), who collected plants on several expeditions in the west. An Internet search will yield lots of information on Fremont's colorful life.

Other Names:
Dwarf Mountain Ragwort

Up to 16″

91

SAW GROUNDSEL
(Senecio serra)
Sunflower Family (Asteraceae)

JFMAMJJASOND

Saw Groundsel *is often seen as a grouping of tall, leafy plants in open forest habitats. It has a large cluster of small yellow flowers and numerous, usually serrated leaves.*

Up to 5′

Large and many-branched diamond-shaped cluster of yellow flowers; each flower up to ½″ across.

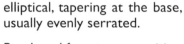

Up to 6″ long and narrowly elliptical, tapering at the base, usually evenly serrated.

Brush and forest communities; low to high elevations.

Northern and central Utah counties; western US.

Serra is the Latin word for "saw." There is an almost identical species, Arrowleaf Groundsel (*Senecio triangularis*), which has leaves that are truncated at the base, giving it the appearance of an arrowhead or long triangle, and has larger teeth at the base of the leaf.

Other Names:

Tall Ragwort

92

COMMON GOLDENROD
(Solidago canadensis)
Sunflower Family (Asteraceae)

JFMAMJJASOND

Common Goldenrod *is a tall, stately plant with a showy, dense cluster of tiny yellow flowers. The stem is leafy all the way to the top. It is just as showy when it has gone to seed (left inset).*

 Pyramid-shaped and many-branched cluster of tiny yellow flowers, usually aligned on the upper side of each branch.

 Up to 5″ long, lance shaped, 3 prominent veins, basal leaves withering at flowering.

 Stream banks, seeps, moist sites; low to moderate elevations.

 All Utah counties; most of North America.

Second Species: Alcove Goldenrod (*Solidago velutina*), shown in the right inset, is not very leafy, has an elongated flower cluster with a graceful curve and flowers aligned on one side of the stem.

Other Names:
Canada Goldenrod
Meadow Goldenrod
(for Common Goldenrod)

Threenerve Goldenrod
Solidago sparsiflora
(for Alcove Goldenrod)

 Up to 5′

93

PARRY'S GOLDENROD
(Solidago parryi)
Sunflower Family (Asteraceae)

JFMAMJJASOND

Parry's Goldenrod *is a higher elevation plant with several yellow daisy-like flowers, nestled in large green bracts that look like small leaves.*

Up to 20″

 Loose cluster of several yellow flowers; each flower up to ¾″.

 Up to 8″ long, elliptical, pointing upward along the stem.

 Forest and alpine tundra communities; moderate to high elevations.

 Most Utah counties; AZ, CO, NM, NV, WY.

Second Species: Low Goldenrod (*Solidago multiradiata*), tends to have more flowers per cluster (left inset) than Parry's Goldenrod, but each flower is smaller and has fewer rays. Also Low Goldenrod has hair at the base of the leaf and on the stem (middle inset), whereas Parry's Goldenrod does not (right inset). Low Goldenrod's range includes all of western US and all of Canada.

Other Names:
Oreochrysum parryi

94

CURLY GUMWEED
(*Grindelia squarrosa*)
Sunflower Family (Asteraceae)

JFMAMJJASOND

Curly Gumweed is a tall, open, weed-like plant with many flower heads. The yellow flowers and the green flower heads with their curly tips are both very resinous and sticky. This combination is pretty unique and makes the plant easily recognizable.

 Yellow, 1–2″ resinous flowers; resinous green flower heads with numerous curlicues.

 Up to 6″ long, sometimes serrated or toothed.

 Drier sites along roads and trails, sagebrush and mountain brush communities; low to moderate elevations.

 All Utah counties; most of North America.

Grindelia is named for David Grindel (1776–1836), a botanist, physician, and pharmacologist in Riga, Estonia. This plant has been used medicinally for treating lung-related problems such as pneumonia, asthma, and bronchitis. However, when grown in selenium rich soil, it has some toxicity.

Other Names:
Curlycup Gumweed, Stickyheads, Resinweed, Tarweed.

Up to 3′

95

HAIRY GOLDENASTER
(*Chrysopsis villosa*)
Sunflower Family (Asteraceae)

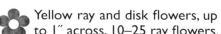

J F M A M J J A S O N D

Hairy Goldenaster *is unusual for an aster because the rays and disk are both yellow. The stems and leaves are both hairy and often sticky with glands.*

Up to 20″

 Yellow ray and disk flowers, up to 1″ across, 10–25 ray flowers.

 Up to 2″ long, elliptical or spatula shaped, hairy and usually sticky or tacky.

 Dry soil and rocky slopes in brush and forest communities; low to high elevations.

 All Utah counties; western North America; southern Canada.

There are two varieties of this species in Utah. The pictures show the variety we see on the Wasatch Front. A southern Utah variety has thicker hair on the leaves and stems, giving them a grayish color.

Other Names:
Heterotheca villosa

96

LONGSTALK SPRING PARSLEY
(*Cymopterus longipes*)
Parsley Family (Apiaceae)

JFMAMJJASOND

Longstalk Spring Parsley *has umbels of yellow flowers that rise above the plant on curved stalks. The basal leaves are compound, and the leaflets overlap each other. This whorl of leaves rises above the ground as the plant matures.*

 Flat-topped umbel of numerous small yellow or whitish flowers.

 Rosette of compound leaves, up to 4″ long. The point where the leaves attach to the stalk appears to be at ground level when the plant is young. As the plant matures and the stalk grows, the attachment point rises above the ground (see inset).

 Sagebrush and mountain brush communities; low to high elevations.

Central and northern Utah; CO, ID, WY.

 Cymopterus is derived from two Greek words meaning "wave" and "wing," referring to the leaves. *Longipes* means "long stalk."

 Up to 12″

97

WESTERN SWEET-CICELY
(*Osmorhiza occidentalis*)
Parsley Family (Apiaceae)

JFMAMJJASOND

 Western Sweet-Cicely *is a robust, leafy herb with tiny yellow flowers arranged in umbels that rise up above the rest of the plant. The foliage is fragrant, and the roots smell like licorice.*

Up to 4′

 Greenish-yellow flowers about ⅛″ across, arranged in a hemispherical compound umbel.

 Compound leaf up to 10″ long, each leaflet often further divided into 3 lance-shaped and serrated leaflets.

 Hillside or stream banks in tall herb or open forest communities; moderate to high elevations.

 Most Utah counties; northwestern North America.

 Osmorhiza is Greek for "odorous root." *Occidentalis* means "of the west."

COMMON DANDELION
(Taraxacum officinale)
Sunflower Family (Asteraceae)

JFMAMJJASOND

This invader from Eurasia may be a hazard in your lawn but is very welcome in the wild. It's one of the first to bloom in the spring and last to quit blooming in the fall. Everyone enjoys blowing on a **dandelion** *puffball.*

 1″ bright yellow flower; numerous ray flowers only, no disk flowers.

 Only basal leaves, up to 16″ long, deeply lobed.

 All communities; low to high elevations.

 All Utah counties; all North America, native of Eurasia.

 Dandelion root has been used as a drug, and the leaves have been eaten as greens for centuries. It is an important food source for some birds and all grazing animals.

Up to 2′

99

PALE AGOSERIS
(*Agoseris glauca*)
Sunflower Family (Asteraceae)

JFMAMJJASOND

This cheerful flower is often mistaken for a true dandelion. However, **Pale Agoseris** *has fewer, broader rays, and the leaves are not deeply lobed like those of a dandelion.*

Up to 2′

 1″ bright yellow flower; ray flowers only, no disk flowers; each petal squared off and with 5 teeth.

 Only basal leaves, up to 10″ long, over 1″ broad, and sometimes toothed or lobed.

 Sagebrush, mountain brush, and alpine meadow communities; low to high elevations.

 Most Utah counties; northern and western North America.

 Agoseris is Greek for "goat chicory." *Glauca* means "blue-gray" and refers to the whitish coating (like you see on plums) on the stem, flower head, or leaves. The stems and leaves have a milky juice that contains a small amount of rubber.

Other Names:
Mountain Dandelion
False Dandelion

100

HOUNDSTONGUE HAWKWEED
(*Hieracium scouleri*)
Sunflower Family (Asteraceae)

JFMAMJJASOND

Houndstongue Hawkweed *is a fascinatingly hairy plant. It tends to grow in clumps and is tall and leggy. The flower resembles a Dandelion or Agoseris.*

 1″ bright yellow flower; ray flowers only, no disk flowers; flower head very hairy.

 Up to 10″ long, elliptical, reducing in size up the stem, very hairy.

 Grass and forest communities; moderate to high elevations.

 Wasatch Front and Uintah mountains; western North America.

 Hieracium is derived from the Greek word for "hawk." Pliny, the Roman, believed that hawks fed on this plant. Hawkweed is one of the first plants to disappear where sheep are foraging.

Up to 3′

YELLOW SALSIFY
(*Tragopogon dubius*)
Sunflower Family (Asteraceae)

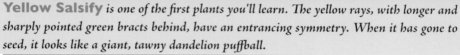

JFMAMJJASOND

Yellow Salsify *is one of the first plants you'll learn. The yellow rays, with longer and sharply pointed green bracts behind, have an entrancing symmetry. When it has gone to seed, it looks like a giant, tawny dandelion puffball.*

Up to 3 ½'

Yellow, up to 1 ½" across, all ray flowers, no disk flowers; the pointed green bracts extend beyond the yellow rays.

Up to 6", narrow, and closely following the stem.

Disturbed sites, roadsides, grass communities; low to high elevations.

All Utah counties; most US states; native to Europe.

Tragopogon is derived from two Greek words meaning "goatsbeard." The roots are edible, and for that reason it was brought to America from Europe.

Other Names:
Goatsbeard

102

WESTERN CONEFLOWER

(*Rudbeckia occidentalis*)

Sunflower Family (Asteraceae)

JFMAMJJASOND

In spite of its dingy color, **Western Coneflower** *is wonderful! The spiral rows of very tiny disk flowers open first at the base, creating a band of yellow that moves up the cone as blooming continues. You'll often see large patches of Coneflower plants. As you can see from the inset, Monarch butterflies enjoy them too.*

 Single, cone-shaped flower terminating each stem; disk flowers only, dark purplish-brown before opening, yellow when open, fading back to dark brown, a whorl of green bracts beneath the cone.

 Up to 8″ long, oval or heart shaped, often serrated or toothed.

 Forest, brush, and grass communities; moderate to high elevations.

 Most Utah counties; western US.

 Coneflower is not usually eaten by grazing animals. If you see a large patch of Coneflower it's often a sign that grazing animals have eaten the competing, tasty plants.

Up to 5′

COBWEBBY GOLDENBUSH
(*Haplopappus macronema*)
Sunflower Family (Asteraceae)

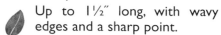

JFMAMJJASOND

Cobwebby Goldenbush *is most often encountered at high elevations on the Wasatch Front. It grows in a wide, mounded shape with numerous yellow flowers and has attractive soft white stems.*

Up to 20″

The inflorescence has a single or several 1″ long, bright yellow flowers per stalk; each flower having 10–25 disk flowers and no ray flowers.

Up to 1½″ long, with wavy edges and a sharp point.

Forest and alpine tundra communities; moderate to high elevations.

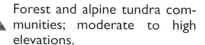

Central and northern Utah counties; western US, excluding AZ, NM.

The common name of "Cobwebby" comes from the dense, short white hair on the stems. This is a useful feature for a high elevation plant because it shields it from the drying effect of strong winds.

Other Names:

Whitestem Goldenbush
Ericameria discoidea

104

RUBBER RABBITBRUSH

(*Chrysothamnus nauseosus*)

Sunflower Family (Asteraceae)

JFMAMJJASOND

Rubber Rabbitbrush *is a grayish green shrub that grows in the same habitat as sagebrush and looks a bit like it from a distance. Until it blooms, that is, and then it's covered with bright golden yellow flowers.*

 Flat-topped clusters of numerous, small, golden yellow flowers with extended stamens creating a feathery look.

 Up to 3″, narrow and straight, usually with some hair.

 Brush communities; low to moderate elevations.

 Most Utah counties; western North America.

 Nauseosus means "nauseating," and in fact, the flowering plant does give off a sickening smell. The associated pollen is a major contributor to allergies. The sap contains small quantities of rubber. It is a complex species with 14 varieties found in Utah. Some authorities have designated these as separate species.

Up to 6′

105

OREGON GRAPE
(*Mahonia repens*)
Barberry Family (Berberidaceae)

JFMAMJJASOND

An evergreen shrub, **Oregon Grape** *is one of the first plants to bloom in the spring. The beautiful yellow flower clusters give way to a blue, grape-looking fruit by mid-summer.*

Up to 12"

 Small bright yellow flowers in showy, dense clusters up to several inches across.

 Same size and appearance as a Concord grape; edible. The plant usually produces fewer (if any) fruit than flowers.

 Up to about 10" long, each leaf contains 3–7 leaflets that can be up to 4" long; hollylike in appearance, a muted green, with some leaves turning reddish colors.

 Dry sites in all communities; low to high elevations.

 All Utah counties; western North America.

 Mahonia is named after Bernard McMahon, an Irish-born horticulturalist who came to America in 1796. He was acquainted with Thomas Jefferson, and it is said that the Lewis and Clark expedition was planned in his home. *Repens* refers to the plant's creeping growth habit.

Other Names: Creeping Mahonia, Creeping Barberry, *Berberis repens*.

106

CONTRA STONESEED
(*Lithospermum ruderale*)
Borage Family (Boraginaceae)

JFMAMJJASOND

Contra Stoneseed *has greenish-yellow flowers nestled in a spray of long, narrow leaves. The stout root produces numerous leafy stems that curve out and upward from the base.*

 Greenish-yellow, up to ½″, attached at the junction of leaf and stem.

 Up to 3″, narrowly lance shaped, crowded at the top of the stem, with short hair on both upper and lower leaf surfaces.

 Brush and forest communities; low to high elevations.

 Most Utah counties; western North America.

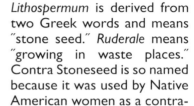 *Lithospermum* is derived from two Greek words and means "stone seed." *Ruderale* means "growing in waste places." Contra Stoneseed is so named because it was used by Native American women as a contraceptive.

Other Names:

Western Stoneseed, Puccoon, Wayside Gromwell.

Up to 2′

107

DYER'S WOAD
(*Isatis tinctoria*)
Mustard Family (Brassicaceae)

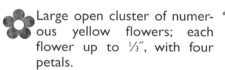

JFMAMJJASOND

Dyer's Woad *puts on quite a show in spring, covering the dry hillsides and the I–15 corridor north of Salt Lake with a blanket of yellow. It is included on the State of Utah's list of noxious weeds.*

Up to 3 ½'

 Large open cluster of numerous yellow flowers; each flower up to ⅓″, with four petals.

Basal leaves up to 6″ long, elliptical; cauline leaves smaller and clasping the stem.

 Roadsides, fallow fields, and dry hillsides; low to moderate elevations.

Northern Utah counties; western and parts of eastern North America; a native of Eurasia.

 Isatis is the ancient Greek name for this plant. *Tinctoria* is often used for any plant that exudes a stain. Do an Internet search on this plant and you'll be amazed at the financial and political impacts it has had throughout history.

WALLFLOWER
(*Erysimum asperum*)
Mustard Family (Brassicaceae)

JFMAMJJASOND

Wallflower *is one of the yellow mustards of spring. Of course spring starts later at higher elevations, and this one grows at all elevations. Look for it scattered sparsely on hillsides.*

 Globular cluster of numerous flowers, which extends in length as the flowers bloom; each flower is 1–2″ across, bright yellow with 4 petals.

 Up to 4″ long, narrow.

 All plant communities; low to high elevations.

 All Utah counties; Rocky Mountains.

 The spring season yields a profusion of blooming white, yellow, and purple plants of the Mustard family. Many domesticated species in the Mustard family include: watercress, radish, turnips, rutabagas, cabbage, and cauliflower.

Other Names:

Western Wallflower

Up to 3′

109

PRINCE'S PLUME
(*Stanleya pinnata*)
Mustard Family (Brassicaceae)

JFMAMJJASOND

Prince's Plume *is more common in southern Utah, but you can find it near the mouth of the southern Wasatch Front canyons. It's quite spectacular!*

Up to 5´

 Extended cylindrical cluster of yellow, tubular flowers with long stamens.

 Up to 7″ long, lance shaped or elliptical, often arranged as parallel rows of leaflets.

 Desert shrub and Pinyon/ Juniper communities; low to moderate elevations.

 Utah county and southward; western US.

 Prince's Plume is one of the many plants growing in Utah that are indicators of selenium in the soil.

110

BLACK TWINBERRY
(*Lonicera involucrata*)
Honeysuckly Family (Caprifoliaceae)

JFMAMJJASOND

Black Twinberry *is a woody shrub with twin, shiny, black berries nestled in bright red bracts. In bloom, the fragrant flowers hide in the foliage and are not very noticeable.*

 Yellow, about ½″ long, developing in pairs and attached to the stem where a leaf attaches.

 Up to 6″ long, broadly elliptical, smooth with some hair along the midvein.

 Moist or wet sites in open forest communities; low to high elevations.

 Almost all Utah counties; western US; all Canada.

 Lonicera is named for Adam Lonitzer (1528–86), a German botanist, physician, and herbalist. *Involucrata* is Latin for "wrapper" and refers to the large, showy bracts that surround the flowers and later the berries. The berries are mildly toxic.

Other Names:

Bear berry honeysuckle

Four-line honeysuckle

Distegia involucrata

Up to
8′

111

OPPOSITE STONECROP
(Sedum debile)
Stonecrop Family (Crassulaceae)

JFMAMJJASOND

Opposite Stonecrop *is true to its name, and is most often seen growing out of some rocky spot. It has clusters of cheerful yellow flowers, and stem leaves that are opposite each other. The short, green succulent leaves at the base will produce next year's flowers.*

Up to
5″

 Loose clusters of several yellow flowers; each flower up to ½″ across, the 5 petals fused together at the base.

 Up to ⅓″, opposite on the stem, cylindrical and succulent in appearance, they wither and fall off during blooming.

 Talus slopes and rock outcrops in mountain brush and forest communities; low to high elevations.

 Most Utah counties; ID, MT, NV, OR, WY.

Second Species: Common Stonecrop (*Sedum lanceolatum*), has leaves that alternate on the stem, and the petals are not fused together. It has a broader range—western North America. The inset picture shows it just about to bloom—the colors are gorgeous!

112

YELLOW SWEETCLOVER
(*Melilotus officinalis*)
Pea Family (Fabaceae)

JFMAMJJASOND

Those masses of green plants with the little yellow flowers that you see along the road at the end of spring are probably **Yellow Sweetclover**. *Some Mustards may look similar, but they have 4 petals. Sweetclover is a true Pea family member and has the typical banner, wings, and keel flower structure.*

 Long clusters of 20–70, yellow, pea-like flowers.

 Leaf stem contains multiple sets of 3 elliptical leaflets.

 Roadsides and open sites; low to moderate elevations.

 Most Utah counties; all North America; native of Europe.

 This European native, and its white-flowered cousin, White Sweetclover (*Melilotus alba*), are forage plants. They are also used in reclamation plantings.

Up to 5´

113

GLACIER LILY
(Erythronium grandiflorum)
Lily Family (Liliaceae)

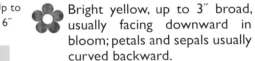

JFMAMJJASOND

For springtime beauty, it's hard to match a **Glacier Lily**. *Look for it in the thousands in the lower canyons, or at the edges of a mountain meadow, shortly after the snow melts.*

Up to 6″

Bright yellow, up to 3″ broad, usually facing downward in bloom; petals and sepals usually curved backward.

Two elliptical leaves per flower stalk, up to 8″ long.

Brush and forest communities; low to high elevations.

 Most Utah counties; western US, excluding AZ, NV.

 Grandiflorum means large-flowered. Native Americans ate all parts of this plant.

Other Names:
Dogtooth-violet
Yellow Avalanche-lily

YELLOW-BELL
(Fritillaria pudica)
Lily Family (Liliaceae)

JFMAMJJASOND

Keep your eyes to the ground in sagebrush country during the first half of spring and you may see these beautiful small **Yellow-bell** *lilies with the rich yellow color.*

 Up to 1″ long, yellow, bell-shaped, and facing downward.

 Two or more slender leaves attached to the stem at or below ground level.

 Sagebrush and open forest communities; low to moderate elevations.

 Wasatch Front counties of Utah; western North America.

 Pudica means "bashful," and refers to how the flower faces downward. The petals close and fade to a rusty red color as the flower ages. The bulbs are 1–6″ below ground.

Other Names:
Yellow Fritillary
Golden Bells

Up to 6″

KING'S YELLOW FLAX
(Linum kingii)
Flax Family (Linaceae)

JFMAMJJASOND

King's Yellow Flax *is a shorter, leafier, more densely flowered plant than its cousin, Blue Flax. We are lucky to have it here since it is found in only a few states other than Utah.*

Up to 12″

 1″ yellow flowers, with 5 petals, tightly grouped in small clusters.

 About 1″, slender, dark green, and numerous.

Brush and forest communities, limestone outcroppings; low to high elevations.

 Most Utah counties; CO, ID, NV, WY.

 Kingii is named after Clarence King (1842–1901) who worked with the geological surveys of the US government. The highest point in Utah, King's Peak, is named after him.

116

BEAUTIFUL BLAZINGSTAR

(*Mentzelia laevicaulis*)

Stickleaf Family (Loasaceae)

JFMAMJJASOND

Beautiful Blazingstar *is a bit scraggly, but it produces the most wonderful, huge lemon-yellow blossoms over a period of several months. The leaves will cling to your clothing.*

 Yellow, up to 6″ across, 5 petals; numerous, long and slender stamens.

 Up to 20″ long, lance shaped, coarsely toothed or lobed.

Brush communities, especially road cuts, steep slopes, and dry streambeds; low elevations.

 Western Utah counties; western US, excluding AZ, NM

 Mentzelia is named after Christian Mentzel (1622–1701), a German botanist. *Laevicaulis* means "smooth stemed" and refers to the lower part of the thick stems.

Up to 4′

117

YELLOW EVENING-PRIMROSE
(*Oenothera flava*)
Evening-primrose Family (Onagraceae)

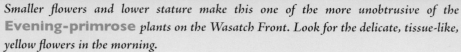

JFMAMJJASOND

Smaller flowers and lower stature make this one of the more unobtrusive of the **Evening-primrose** *plants on the Wasatch Front. Look for the delicate, tissue-like, yellow flowers in the morning.*

Up to
8″

  Pure yellow flowers, up to 2″ broad, fading to a reddish or bronze color; 4 heart-shaped petals, 4 greenish sepals bent backward.

 Up to 10″ or more, slender, with a lot of variation in surface and edges.

 Brush and meadow communities; low to high elevations.

 All Utah counties; western North America.

 Flava comes from the Latin word for "pure yellow." The Evening-primrose family is not related to the true Primrose family, except in so far as some members have a similar fragrance.

HOOKER'S EVENING-PRIMROSE

(*Oenothera elata*)

Evening-primrose Family (Onagraceae)

JFMAMJJASOND

Hooker's Evening-primrose *has very large, pure yellow flowers that flap delicately in the slightest breeze. The plant has a leggy, open appearance.*

 Yellow, up to 4″ across; petals heart shaped, delicate, fading to orange or purple after one day of blooming.

 Up to 10″, elliptical with pointed ends, mainly cauline.

 Moist sites in brush and forest communities; low to high elevations.

 Most Utah counties; western US.

 Oenothera is Greek for "wine imbibe" and was named because a related European plant was thought to induce a taste for wine. *Elata* means "tall."

Up to 5′

SULFUR BUCKWHEAT
(*Eriogonum umbellatum*)
Buckwheat Family (Polygonaceae)

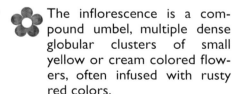

JFMAMJJASOND

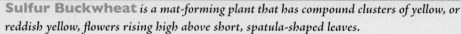

Sulfur Buckwheat *is a mat-forming plant that has compound clusters of yellow, or reddish yellow, flowers rising high above short, spatula-shaped leaves.*

Up to 2´

 The inflorescence is a compound umbel, multiple dense globular clusters of small yellow or cream colored flowers, often infused with rusty red colors.

 Up to 1˝ long, nearly as broad, oval or spatula-shaped.

 Sagebrush and mountain brush communities; moderate to high elevations.

 Most Utah counties; western North America.

Umbellatum refers to the shape of the inflorescence. This species has a huge amount of variation in its physical characteristics.

120

PLANTAIN BUTTERCUP
(*Ranunculus alismifolius*)
Buttercup Family (Ranunculaceae)

JFMAMJJASOND

The amazing carpet of bright yellow you see on a mountain meadow soon after the snow has melted is probably **Plantain Buttercup**.

 Shiny yellow, ¾″ flower, 3–10 or more petals.

 Up to 4″ long, usually lance shaped, and not divided like most other Buttercup species.

 Wet meadows, stream banks; moderate to high elevations.

 Mountainous counties of Utah; western North America.

 Alismifolius means "leaves like Alisma." Alisma is a genus of plants in the Water Plantain family.

Other Names:
Meadow Buttercup

Up to 18″

ALPINE BUTTERCUP
(*Ranunculus adoneus*)
Buttercup Family (Ranunculaceae)

JFMAMJJASOND

At timberline and above, you'll likely see one or both of the Buttercups on this page and the following page. They both have big, shiny, bright yellow petals. **Alpine Buttercup** has leaves that are divided into very slender leaflets.

Up to 12″

 Shiny yellow, 1″ flower, 5 sepals, 5–12 petals.

 Up to 2″ long, divided several times into very narrow leaflets.

Talus slopes, meadows, open forest communities; high elevations.

 Wasatch and Uintah mountains; CO, ID, MT, NV, WY.

 Deer, elk, and some burrowing rodents eat the foliage. Mice and chipmunks eat the seeds.

Second Species: Subalpine Buttercup (*Ranunculus eschscholtzii*), shown in the inset, has leaves divided into three wide leaflets.

122

YELLOW COLUMBINE
(Aquilegia flavescens)
Buttercup Family (Ranunculaceae)

JFMAMJJASOND

The tall slender flower stalks of Yellow Columbine *rise high above the attractive leaves at the base. Usually with pale yellow flowers, it's a treat to find one with some pinkish color. Just about every mountain stream you cross will have a patch of Yellow Columbine.*

 Pale yellow, sometimes pinkish, 2″ flowers, 5 petals with hooked spurs, 5 sepals bent backward; one or several flowers on each stem.

 Compound leaf up to 15″ long, usually divided twice into 3 leaflets.

 Streams, seeps, and wet areas; low to high elevations.

 Central mountainous spine of Utah; northwestern North America.

 Aquilegia comes from the Latin word for "eagle" because the shape of the petal resembles an eagle's talon. *Flavescens* means "yellowish."

Up to 3′

123

SLENDER CINQUEFOIL
(Potentilla gracilis)
Rose Family (Rosaceae)

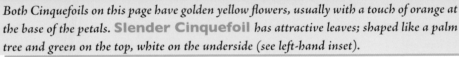

JFMAMJJASOND

Both Cinquefoils on this page have golden yellow flowers, usually with a touch of orange at the base of the petals. **Slender Cinquefoil** has attractive leaves; shaped like a palm tree and green on the top, white on the underside (see left-hand inset).

Up to 2′

 Golden yellow, 1″ flower with 5 sepals and 5 petals; in loose clusters that can have numerous flowers.

 Up to 12″ long, divided into 5–9 leaflets that are often green above but gray underneath because the underside is covered with short white hair.

 Meadows, brush, and forest communities; low to high elevations.

 Most Utah counties; western North America.

Second Species: Wedge-leaf Cinquefoil (*Potentilla diversifolia*) is generally a shorter plant, with fewer flowers, and a wedge-shaped leaf (see right-hand inset).

124

SHRUBBY CINQUEFOIL
(Potentilla fruticosa)
Rose Family (Rosaceae)

JFMAMJJASOND

This **Cinquefoil** *is very easy to recognize because it is the only one that is shrubby. It has shreddy bark and numerous, but not dense, single yellow flowers. You may also recognize it as a common landscaping plant.*

 Bright yellow, 1″ flower with 5 sepals and 5 petals.

 Up to 2″ long, divided into 3–7 leaflets.

 Meadows, brush, and forest communities; low to high elevations.

 Most Utah counties; North America except for southeastern US.

 Potentilla possibly comes from the Latin word for "powerful" because of the medicinal properties of some species. *Fruticosa* means "small and shrubby." The common name, Cinquefoil, literally means "five leaves," referring to the number of leaflets.

Other Names:
Yellow Rose, Tundra Rose, Widdy, Golden Hardhack, *Dasiphora fruticosa.*

Up to 3′

125

ROSS' AVENS
(*Geum rossii*)
Rose Family (Rosaceae)

JFMAMJJASOND

Ross' Avens *is a short, high-elevation plant with a mass of dark green leaves at the base, each leaf divided into many leaflets. The buttery yellow flowers resemble the Cinquefoil flowers shown on the previous two pages.*

Up to 7″

 Yellow, up to ¾″ across, 5 petals and 5 (greenish) sepals, numerous stamens; one to several flowers per stem.

 Basal leaf compound, up to 15″, with 15–31 leaflets that are toothed or lobed; cauline leaves few and small.

 Alpine meadows, rocky slopes; high elevations.

 Mountainous Utah counties; western US and Alaska; northern Canada.

 Rossii is named for the Scottish explorer, John Ross (1777–1856), the first person to reach the magnetic North Pole.

126

GORDON'S IVESIA
(Ivesia gordonii)
Rose Family (Rosaceae)

JFMAMJJASOND

Gordon's Ivesia *is common throughout Utah, and those on the Wasatch Front are particularly robust. Look for a healthy clump of finely divided leaves at the base and tight clusters of yellow flowers at the end of a reddish stem.*

 Dense, rounded cluster of 10–20 yellow flowers, one or several clusters terminating each long red stem.

 Compound basal leaf, up to 10″, with 20–50 leaflets.

 Alpine sites, rocky meadows; moderate to high elevations.

 Most Utah counties; western US.

 Ivesia is named for Eli Ives (1779–1861), a professor at Yale University who established a botanical garden as part of the medical school. *Gordonii* is named after Alexander Gordon, an English horticulturalist who made two trips through the American West in the 1840s.

Up to 12″

127

BITTERBRUSH
(*Purshia tridentata*)
Rose Family (Rosaceae)

JFMAMJJASOND

Bitterbrush *and Cliffrose (next page) are the two Purshia species you'll find on the Wasatch Front. Both are shrubs with numerous yellow flowers and leaves that are green on the top and gray underneath. Bitterbrush tends to be shorter and has leaves with three teeth on the end.*

Up to 6′

 Pale yellow, ½″ flower.

 Up to 1″ long, wedge shaped, with 3 teeth on the end, hairy, green on top, grayish underneath.

 Dry sites in sagebrush and mountain brush communities; low to moderate elevations.

 All Utah counties; western United States.

 Purshia is named after Frederick Pursh, one of the first to work on the plants brought back from the Lewis and Clark expedition. *Tridentata* means "three toothed." It is an important browse plant for deer.

Other Names:
Antelope Bitterbrush
Buckbrush

128

CLIFF-ROSE
(Purshia mexicana)
Rose Family (Rosaceae)

JFMAMJJASOND

Cliff-rose *is similar to its cousin, Bitterbrush, on the previous page. Cliff-rose tends to be taller, has leaves with five lobes, and long feathery styles attached to the seeds.*

 Pale yellow, ¾″ flower; forming long, feathery styles as the flower ages.

 Up to ¾″ long, wedge shaped, with 5 lobes, hairy, green on top, grayish underneath.

 Dry sites in sagebrush and mountain brush communities; low to moderate elevations.

 Most Utah counties; western United States.

 Mexicana means "means of or from Mexico." This plant was first collected by Howard Stansbury, a surveyor and explorer, in 1850.

Up to 10′

Other Names:
Purshia stansburiana
Cowania mexicana

129

COMMON MONKEYFLOWER
(*Mimulus guttatus*)
Snapdragon Family (Scrophulariaceae)

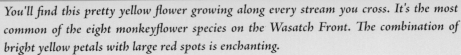

JFMAMJJASOND

You'll find this pretty yellow flower growing along every stream you cross. It's the most common of the eight monkeyflower species on the Wasatch Front. The combination of bright yellow petals with large red spots is enchanting.

Up to 3′

 Up to 1½″ long; yellow petals with red spots and yellow hair on the lower lip, usually 5 or more flower heads per stalk.

 Up to 3″ long, broadly oval, often serrated, in pairs on the stem, and with prominent veins.

 Marshy areas, seeps, springs, stream banks; low to high elevations.

 All Utah counties; western North America

 Mimulus possibly comes from the Latin word for "actor" or "mimic" because the flower resembles the masks they wore. *Guttatus* means "a drop-like spot" in Latin and refers to the red spots on the lower petals.

Other Names:

Golden Monkeyflower
Yellow Monkeyflower
Mimulus luteus

JFMAMJJASOND

Subalpine Monkeyflower *resembles its cousin, Common Monkeyflower on the previous page. However, it has bigger, but fewer, flower heads on each stalk. Look for it at higher elevations.*

 Up to 2″ long; yellow petals, with red spots and yellow hair on the lower lip; usually 1–3 flower heads per stalk.

 Usually about to 1″ long, oval or diamond shaped, often serrated.

 Wet places on hillsides and forest communities; moderate to high elevations.

 Central and southern Wasatch Front, Uintahs; western North America.

 Tilingii was named for Heinrich Tiling (1818–71) who worked for the Russian-American company in Sitka and collected plants in CA and NV.

Other Names:

Tiling's Monkeyflower
Mountain Monkeyflower

Up to 10″

131

TOLMIE'S OWL CLOVER
(*Orthocarpus tolmiei*)
Snapdragon Family (Scrophulariaceae)

JFMAMJJASOND

In late summer this short plant with yellow flower clusters on top is common at higher elevations. Examine the little hook at the top lip of the flower; it looks like the head of a small bird.

Up to 12″

 Yellow, sometimes purple-tipped; arranged in a compact cluster surrounded by yellowish or greenish bracts.

 Up to 2″ long; narrow, lance shaped.

 Mountain brush and forest communities; moderate to high elevations.

 Northern Utah counties; ID, WY.

 Tolmiei is named for William Tolmie (1812–86), a physician with the Hudson Bay Company in Fort Vancouver. Owl's Clover, as a member of the Snapdragon family, is not a true clover, which are members of the Pea family.

132

DALMATIAN TOADFLAX
(*Linaria dalmatica*)
Snapdragon Family (Scrophulariaceae)

JFMAMJJASOND

Dalmatian Toadflax *looks very much like a tall version of the snapdragon plants in your garden. The flowers are yellow, sometimes with orange hair on the lower portion of the corolla. The stems are stout and waxy, and the lower leaves clasp the stem.*

 Spike-shaped cluster, loosely packed with yellow flowers, each having a spur and a white or orange bearded throat.

 Up to 1½" long, oval, lower leaves clasping the stem.

 Brush and forest communities; low to high elevations.

 Northern Utah counties; most of North America; native of Eurasia.

 A native of Eurasia, Dalmatian Toadflax has spread throughout North America. The State of Utah considers it a noxious weed.

Second Species:
Butter-and-Eggs (*Linaria vulgaris*), also a noxious weed and Eurasian native, has narrower leaves that do not clasp the stem and a more tightly packed flower cluster.

Up to 4′

133

WOOLLY MULLEIN
(*Verbascum thapsus*)
Snapdragon Family (Scrophulariaceae)

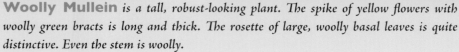

JFMAMJJASOND

Woolly Mullein *is a tall, robust-looking plant. The spike of yellow flowers with woolly green bracts is long and thick. The rosette of large, woolly basal leaves is quite distinctive. Even the stem is woolly.*

Up to 8'

Spike-shaped cluster up to 12″ long; densely packed with yellow flowers.

Basal leaves up to 20″, elliptical, densely covered with short hair; cauline leaves smaller.

Open sites in brush and forest communities; low to high elevations.

All Utah counties; North America; native of Eurasia.

Although a native of Eurasia, Woolly Mullein has spread throughout North America. You can even find it in Greenland! Mullein is used for a variety of purposes in herbal medicines.

NUTTALL'S VIOLET

(*Viola nuttallii*)

Violet Family (Violaceae)

JFMAMJJASOND

Two beautiful little yellow violets are common on the Wasatch Front. Both have the typical violet shape, yellow petals, and purple "guidelines" for insects on the petals.

 Up to ¾" long, with yellow petals having purple veins.

 Up to 3" long, up to 1½" broad.

Brush and forest communities; low to high elevations.

 Most Utah counties; Rocky Mountain and Plains states.

 Nuttallii is named for Thomas Nuttall (1786–1859) a curator of the Harvard Botanical Gardens who traveled overland to Oregon in 1834.

Second Species:
Pine Violet (*Viola purpurea*), shown in the inset, has toothed leaves with purple veins.

Up to 10"

135

GIANT LOMATIUM

(*Lomatium dissectum*)

Parsley Family (Apiaceae)

JFMAMJJASOND

Giant Lomatium *often appears in clumps or colonies on the edges of the forest. The greenish or yellowish flower cluster is small and compact when the flower stem first appears at the base of the plant. As the stem grows tall, the flower cluster expands in size, eventually producing seeds with two flat wings.*

Up to 4′

 Large compound umbel of small greenish, yellowish, or purplish flowers.

 Compound leaf, resembling Italian parsley (same plant family); basal leaf often over 12″ long, cauline leaves much smaller.

 Shady or moist spots in sagebrush and forest communities; low to moderate elevations.

 Most Utah counties; western North America.

 Lomatium is derived from the Greek word for "bordered," and refers to the wings on the seeds. *Dissectum* means "dissected" and refers to how the compound leaf is divided several times into small leaflets.

Other Names:

Fernleaf Lomatium

Fernleaf Biscuitroot

136

BIG SAGEBRUSH
(*Artemisia tridentata*)
Sunflower Family (Asteraceae)

JFMAMJJASOND

Big Sagebrush *is a woody shrub that can grow quite tall. The picture above shows the whole plant in bloom, but the spiky flower clusters (inset) are unobtrusive, and from a distance look like an extension of the branches.*

 Spiky clusters of numerous, tiny flowers with greenish bracts.

 Up to 2″, gray-green, wedge shaped, 3–5 teeth on the leaf tip.

 Brush communities; low to moderate elevations.

 All Utah counties; western North America.

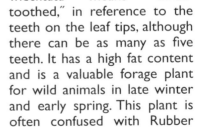 *Tridentata* means "three-toothed," in reference to the teeth on the leaf tips, although there can be as many as five teeth. It has a high fat content and is a valuable forage plant for wild animals in late winter and early spring. This plant is often confused with Rubber Rabbitbrush in the yellow flower section.

Up to 8′

137

ELKWEED
(*Swertia radiata*)
Gentian Family (Gentianaceae)

JFMAMJJASOND

Elkweed *is tall and robust with long ascending leaves. About 80 percent of its height is covered with numerous buds and green-white flowers with purple spots and glands. Take time to look closely at these intricate flowers.*

Up to 7´

 1–2˝ greenish flowers, with purple spots and two hairy purple glands on each petal, and with a large green ovary in the center.

 Up to 20˝, elliptical.

 Mountain brush and forest communities; moderate to high elevations.

 All Utah counties; western US.

 Swertia is named for Emmanuel Sweert (1552–1612), a Dutch botanist. *Radiata* means "spreading out from a center point." Elk like to eat the new leaves at the base of this plant.

Other Names:
Monument Plant
Green Gentian
Frasera speciosa

138

FALSE HELLEBORE
(*Veratrum californicum*)
Lily Family (Liliaceae)

JFMAMJJASOND

You'll usually find **False Hellebore,** *or Skunk Cabbage, growing in large patches. Just before it blooms, enjoy the broad leaves with their many color striations. In bloom, it stands above everything around it.*

 The flower cluster expands up to 2´ as the flowers bloom; clusters of numerous greenish-white flowers with green stripes.

 Numerous, up to 12˝ long, almost as broad, clasping the stem, often with alternating bands of light and dark colored veins.

 Meadows and stream banks; moderate to high elevations.

 Most Utah counties; western US.

 Veratrum is Latin for "dark roots." The plant contains alkaloids that have been used medicinally. When eaten by pregnant sheep it causes abortions or birth defects.

Other Names:
Skunk Cabbage
Corn Lily

Up to 7´

139

FENDLER'S MEADOWRUE
(Thalictrum fendleri)
Buttercup Family (Ranunculaceae)

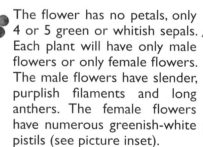

J F M A M J J A S O N D

Fendler's Meadowrue *is a delicate plant with fern-like leaves and purplish-green stems. The numerous long stamens on the male plants hang down and blow in the slightest breeze, like tiny wind-chimes.*

Up to 5′

 The flower has no petals, only 4 or 5 green or whitish sepals. Each plant will have only male flowers or only female flowers. The male flowers have slender, purplish filaments and long anthers. The female flowers have numerous greenish-white pistils (see picture inset).

Each leaf contains three leaflets, each divided once more into another set of 3 leaflets.

 Open forest or mountain brush communities; low to high elevations.

All Utah counties; western US.

Fendleri is named after Augustus Fendler, a German plant collector who joined the American soldiers sent to Santa Fe to fight the Mexicans in 1846.

STINGING NETTLE
(Urtica dioica)
Nettle Family (Urticaceae)

JFMAMJJASOND

Stinging Nettle *is a hiker's occupational hazard as it often borders a mountain trail. Learn to recognize and avoid the long, serrated leaves radiating out from the tall stems.*

 Twisted clusters of inconspicuous flowers arising out of the node where the leaf joins the stem.

 Up to 7" long, lance shaped, coarsely serrated, underside covered with stinging hairs.

 Both moist and dry sites; low to moderate elevations.

 Most Utah counties; all North America.

 Urtica means "I burn." The stinging hairs inject formic acid, which creates a burning sensation that can last from minutes to days. Bees and ants use formic acid as a defense. The Latin word for ant is "formica."

Up to 6'

141

CHICORY
(*Cichorium intybus*)
Sunflower Family (Asteraceae)

JFMAMJJASOND

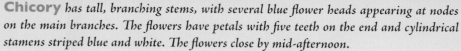

Chicory *has tall, branching stems, with several blue flower heads appearing at nodes on the main branches. The flowers have petals with five teeth on the end and cylindrical stamens striped blue and white. The flowers close by mid-afternoon.*

Up to 4′

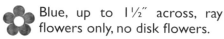

Blue, up to 1½″ across, ray flowers only, no disk flowers.

Up to 8″ long, scalloped and toothed edges, much smaller on the upper stems.

Roadsides and disturbed sites; low elevations.

Almost all Utah counties; all North America; native of Eurasia.

Cichorium is derived from the Greek name for one species of this genus. *Intybus* derives from the Egyptian word for "January," the month it was customarily eaten. Dried chicory roots, ground and roasted, are a common ingredient in coffee substitutes. Chicory is a highly nutritious forage plant. A close relative, endive, is cultivated as a salad plant.

142

WASATCH BLUEBELL
(Mertensia brevistyla)
Borage Family (Boraginaceae)

J F M A M J J A S O N D

As it carpets the ground underneath the oaks with its pretty blue flowers, Wasatch Bluebell *announces the beginning of the blooming season on the* Wasatch Front.

 Deep blue (sometimes white), ¼″ flowers, 5 petals fused together into a bell shape.

 Up to 5″ long, oblong.

 Sagebrush and forest communities; moderate to high elevations.

 Mountain counties of Utah; CO, ID, NV, WY.

 Mertensia is named for a German Botanist Franz Mertens (1764–1831). *Brevistyla* refers to the short style, which is hidden down in the tube of the flower.

Other Names:
Shortstyle Bluebell

Up to 12″

143

MOUNTAIN BLUEBELL
(*Mertensia ciliata*)
Borage Family (Boraginaceae)

JFMAMJJASOND

Mountain Bluebell *is a tall leafy plant with the pretty little blue and pink bells hanging down. You'll often see large patches of it in meadows and on mountainsides.*

Up to 4′

 Blue, fading to pink as they age, ½″ flowers with 5 petals fused together into a bell-shape.

 Up to 6″ long, variously shaped, prominent midvein and lateral veins.

 Mountain brush and forest communities; moderate to high elevations.

 Mountain counties of Utah; western US.

 Ciliata refers to the whitish fringe you see on the calyx lobes of each flower.

Other Names:
Tall Fringed Bluebell

Second Species: You'll encounter two other, very similar bluebell species on the Wasatch Front. Tall Bluebell (*Mertensia arizonica*) has longer (over 5 mm) calyx lobes. Western Bluebell (*Mertensia oblongifolia*) is shorter than the other two, and does not have prominent lateral veins in the cauline leaves.

144

SHOWY STICKSEED
(Hackelia floribunda)
Borage Family (Boraginaceae)

Showy Stickseed *is very pretty and produces a bluish tinge to large areas of open forest in the early summer. Stickseeds resemble true Forget-Me-Nots (genus Mysotis), which are rare on the Wasatch Front.*

 Each plant usually has many flower clusters. Each cluster has many sky blue, ¼″ flowers with 5 petals and a white and yellow center.

 Up to 6″ long, slender and pointed.

 Sagebrush and forest communities; low to high elevations.

 Most counties of Utah; western North America.

 Hackelia is named after Josef Hackel (1783–1869), a Czech botanist. *Floribunda* means "having abundant flowers."

Second Species: Small-flowered Stickseed (*Hackelia micrantha*), shown in the two inset pictures, has fewer and smaller flowers, more stems, and more prickles on the nutlet.

Up to 4′

145

BLUE FLAX
(*Linum perenne*)
Flax Family (Linaceae)

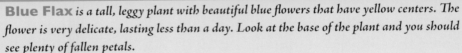

JFMAMJJASOND

Blue Flax *is a tall, leggy plant with beautiful blue flowers that have yellow centers. The flower is very delicate, lasting less than a day. Look at the base of the plant and you should see plenty of fallen petals.*

Up to
2 ½"

Up to 1", deep to pale blue, with yellow centers, 5 petals, stamens, and styles.

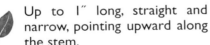

Up to 1" long, straight and narrow, pointing upward along the stem.

Brush and forest communities; low to high elevations.

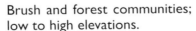

All Utah counties; central and western North America.

Linum comes from the old Greek word for flax. *Perenne* is Latin for perennial. Several Native American tribes used this plant for making rope. Plants from the flax family were used to make the wrappings for Egyptian mummies and are the source of linseed oil.

Other Names:
Lewis Flax
Prairie Flax
Adenolinum lewisii

146

PRETTY JACOB'S LADDER
(Polemonium pulcherrimum)
Phlox Family (Polemoniaceae)

JFMAMJJASOND

Pretty Jacob's ladder has attractive foliage, beautiful clusters of blue-violet flowers with yellow centers and purple guidelines. But don't step on it! The crushed leaves have a skunk-like odor.

 Loose or tight clusters; blue to violet, ½″, bell-shaped flowers with yellow centers, often with distinct purple insect guidelines.

 Up to 8″ long, 7–25 lance shaped or elliptical leaflets in two parallel rows.

 Forest and grass communities; moderate to high elevations.

 Most Utah counties; western North America.

 Pulcherrimum means "prettiest." The plants in the Polemonium genus are collectively referred to as Jacob's ladder. Compare Pretty Jacob's ladder to Leafy Jacobsladder in the white flower section.

Up to 10″

147

WASATCH PENSTEMON
(*Penstemon cyananthus*)
Snapdragon Family (Scrophulariaceae)

JFMAMJJASOND

Wasatch Penstemon *is spectacular! It has several dense clusters of beautiful, deep sky blue flowers. You'll find lots of it on the Wasatch Front in late spring and early summer.*

Up to 3′

 2–10 clusters; each cluster has 1–7 blue flowers with tufts of yellow hair on the staminode.

 Up to 5″, broadly lance shaped, leaf edges often crinkled or wavy.

 Mountain brush and forest communities; moderate to high elevations.

 Wasatch Front; ID, MT, WY.

Second Species: Glabrous Penstemon (*Penstemon subglaber*), shown in the inset, is similar to Wasatch Penstemon in appearance, flowering time, habitat, and range. Look for Glabrous Penstemon's glandular spots, like tiny glistening hairs, on the calyx and its attachment to the stem.

148

LOW PENSTEMON
(*Penstemon humilis*)
Snapdragon Family (Scrophulariaceae)

J F M A M J J A S O N D

Low Penstemon *is widespread, and you shouldn't have any trouble locating one of its many varieties. It's compact, almost mat-forming, with blue flower clusters rising proudly above the foliage.*

 3–10 clusters; each cluster has 4–10, ½″ blue flowers, tufts of golden hair on the staminode, dark purple insect guidelines, and often red stems.

 Basal leaves up to 4″, oval or elliptic; cauline leaves up to 2″, narrowly oblong or lance shaped.

 Many plant communities; low to high elevations.

 All of Utah except the southeast; western US.

 Humilis means "low-growing" and is related to the word "humble."

 Up to 12″

149

SHOWY DAISY
(*Erigeron speciosus*)
Sunflower Family (Asteraceae)

JFMAMJJASOND

Showy Daisy *is aptly named! It produces numerous beautiful purple flowers with yellow centers. It has a long blooming season and a broad habitat. It will be a frequent companion on your hikes in the canyons and mountains of the Wasatch Front.*

Up to 3′

 Purple, pink, or white, up to 1¾″ across, 75–150 very slender rays, dark yellow disk flowers, up to 15 flowers per stem.

 Up to 5″, oval, elliptical, or lance shaped.

Brush, forest, and meadow communities; low to high elevations.

 All Utah counties; western North America.

 Speciosus means "showy." Showy Daisy can be confused with Wandering Daisy on the next page. Showy Daisy will be leafy all the way up the stem, and will have over 75 petals (ray flowers).

Other Names:
Oregon Daisy
Oregon Fleabane
Aspen Fleabane
Showy Fleabane
Pretty Daisy

WANDERING DAISY

(Erigeron peregrinus)

Sunflower Family (Asteraceae)

JFMAMJJASOND

Wandering Daisy *can be found from Alaska down to New Mexico. It has small, beautiful, lavender-purple rays and a golden-yellow disk. Look for it at elevations above 7500' in mid to late summer.*

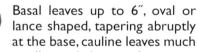

Up to 1¾" across, usually 1–6 flowers per stem; 30–75 purple ray flowers, yellow disk flowers.

Basal leaves up to 6", oval or lance shaped, tapering abruptly at the base, cauline leaves much smaller and clasping the stem.

Aspen and forest communities; moderate to high elevations.

Mountainous Utah counties; western North America.

One interpretation of the word *peregrinus* is "wandering." Wandering Daisy can be confused with Showy Daisy on the previous page. Wandering Daisy will have only very small leaves on the upper stem, and will have fewer than 75 petals (ray flowers).

Other Names:

Strange Daisy
Subalpine Fleabane

Up to 2 ½'

151

LEAFYBRACT ASTER
(*Aster foliaceus*)
Sunflower Family (Asteraceae)

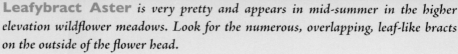

J F M A M J J A S O N D

Leafybract Aster *is very pretty and appears in mid-summer in the higher elevation wildflower meadows. Look for the numerous, overlapping, leaf-like bracts on the outside of the flower head.*

Up to 2 ½'

 Flat-topped cluster of up to 20 flowers; each flower up to 2" across, cupped by many leaf-like green bracts.

Up to 6" long at the base, upper leaves smaller, narrow, and pointed.

Mountain brush and forest communities; moderate to high elevations.

 Wasatch Front; western US.

 Foliaceus means "leafy."

Other Names:
Symphyotrichum foliaceum

152

PACIFIC ASTER

(Aster ascendens)

Sunflower Family (Asteraceae)

JFMAMJJASOND

Pacific Aster *begins to appear in mid-summer when you'll see pale-colored clumps of them along the roads and trails in the canyons. Stop and take a look at these graceful flowers.*

 Each flower head has 15–40 ray flowers, purple, pinkish, rarely white, up to 1½″ across; disk flowers yellow, fading to reddish-brown.

 Lower leaves up to 6″ long, smaller at top, narrow, with stiff short hair on the leaf edges.

 Most communities; low to moderate elevations.

 All Utah counties; western North America.

 Pacific Aster has a lot of variability. It can appear as a short plant with just a few flowers or as a tall plant with numerous flowers that rise to about the same height and have leafy flower heads.

Other Names:

Western Aster
Symphyotrichum ascendens

Up to 3′

153

HOARY ASTER
(*Machaeranthera canescens*)
Sunflower Family (Asteraceae)

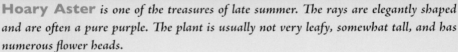

JFMAMJJASOND

Hoary Aster *is one of the treasures of late summer. The rays are elegantly shaped and are often a pure purple. The plant is usually not very leafy, somewhat tall, and has numerous flower heads.*

Up to 2´

15–25 ray flowers, purple, pinkish, or white, up to 1˝ across, yellow disk flowers; flower head often sticky or tacky, bracts green-tipped and often bent downwards.

Basal leaves usually dried up by blooming time; upper leaves up to 4˝ long, stiff hair on leaf edges, often sticky or tacky.

Desert brush, sagebrush, forest, and alpine meadow communities; low to high elevations.

Most Utah counties; central and western North America.

Machaeranthera is Greek for ˝sword-like anthers,˝ referring to the long, triangular-tipped anthers. Examine a mature flower; the anthers will look like Roman short swords jutting above the disk. *Canescens* means ˝covered with short hair.˝ Hoary Aster varies considerably in some of its features, including hairiness.

154

CANADA THISTLE
(Cirsium arvense)
Sunflower Family (Asteraceae)

JFMAMJJASOND

Canada Thistle *often grows in large patches and has beautiful, purple, pompom-shaped flowers that are pleasantly fragrant.*

 Pinkish-purple, all disk flowers, fragrant, spiny tips on flower head bracts; a single plant has either all male or all female flowers.

 Up to 6″ long, half as wide, lobed and toothed, with spiny edges

 Roadsides, fields; aspen communities; low to moderate elevations.

 All Utah counties; North America; native of Eurasia.

 The State of Utah has declared Canada Thistle a noxious weed. Its deep rootstock makes it hard to kill.

Other Names:
Breea arvensis
Serratula arvensis

Up to 3′

155

MUSK MUSTARD
(*Chorispora tenella*)
Mustard Family (Brassicaceae)

JFMAMJJASOND

Musk Mustard *blankets empty lots, fallow fields, and roadsides with a purple haze. It's one of the more showy of the numerous Mustard plants that bloom in the spring.*

Up to 20″

 A spiky cluster that extends as the flower grows; flowers pinkish-purple, up to 1″ across, with a musky odor; reddish or purplish sepals with glandular spots.

 Up to 3 long, mostly cauline, usually lobed and/or serrated.

 Roadsides, fields, and disturbed sites; low to moderate elevations.

 All Utah counties; most of the US.

 Chorispora is derived from two Greek words and means "separate seeds," in reference to the partition inside the seed pods that separates the seeds. *Tenella* is Latin for "dainty" or "quite delicate."

Other Names:
Crossflower
Purple Mustard

156

TEASEL
(*Dipsacus sylvestris*)
Teasel Family (Dipsacaceae)

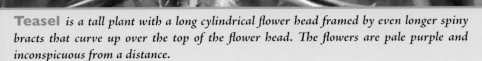

J F M A M J J A S O N D

Teasel is a tall plant with a long cylindrical flower head framed by even longer spiny bracts that curve up over the top of the flower head. The flowers are pale purple and inconspicuous from a distance.

 Dense cylindrical head, up to 4″ long, pale purple flowers, interspersed with spiny bracts.

 Up to 2′ long, lance shaped, prickly along the veins.

 Moist roadsides or hillsides, ditch banks, marshes; low to moderate elevations.

 Wasatch Front; most of the US; native of Europe.

 This European native is considered a noxious weed in some states. It dries intact, and the dry stalks can last a year or more in the open.

Up to 7′

Other Names:
Fuller's Teasel
Dipsacus fullonum

157

ALFALFA
(*Medicago sativa*)
Pea Family (Fabaceae)

JFMAMJJASOND

If you see a field of green hay, go take a look. It's probably **Alfalfa**. *This plant has escaped cultivation and can be found at the lower elevations of most mountain trails. The flower clusters are beautiful!*

Up to 4′

 Long clusters of 5–25, deep to very pale purple, pea-like flowers.

 Leaf stem contains multiple sets of 3 elliptical leaflets.

 Roadsides and open sites; low to moderate elevations.

 All Utah counties; all North America; native of Eurasia.

 This Eurasian native has been used for various purposes since ancient times. An Internet search will yield volumes of information about it.

SILVERY LUPINE
(*Lupinus argenteus*)
Pea Family (Fabaceae)

JFMAMJJASOND

A hillside covered with **Silvery Lupine,** *interspersed with the red, white, and yellow colors of other wildflowers is breathtaking! Silvery Lupine is the most common and widespread lupine in Utah. It varies greatly in size, color, and hairiness.*

 Borne in a cylindrical cluster up to 10″ long, each with numerous purple, blue, white, or pink flowers; each flower is about ½″ and pea-like, often with a white or yellow spot on the banner.

 Palm-shaped compound leaf with 6–9 leaflets; each leaflet up to 4″ long, spatula shaped, often folded.

 Open sites in most communities; low to high elevations.

 All Utah counties; western North America.

 Lupinus is derived from the Latin word for "wolf." It was believed that Lupine plants robbed the soil because they are often seen growing on poor ground. In reality Lupines can use nitrogen in the atmosphere to make their own fertilizer, and they actually improve the soil.

Up to 3′

159

WESTERN WATERLEAF
(*Hydrophyllum occidentale*)
Waterleaf Family (Hydrophyllaceae)

JFMAMJJASOND

The two Waterleaf species described on this page are often found growing out of the leaves carpeting the ground under oak trees. **Western Waterleaf** *has lavender colored flower clusters that rise up above its foliage.*

Up to 2′

  Globular clusters of ¼″, lavender to white, bell-shaped flowers with stamens that stick out beyond the corolla.

 Up to 10″, divided 7–15 times, soft with tiny hair that lies flat on the leaf surface.

 Mountain brush and Pinyon/Juniper communities; low to high elevations.

 Western Utah counties; AZ, CA, ID, NV, OR.

Second Species: Ballhead Waterleaf also known as Capitate Waterleaf (*Hydrophyllum capitatum*) is shown in the inset. It has globular clusters of flowers that are shorter than the plant's foliage.

160

CARSON'S PHACELIA
(Phacelia linearis)
Waterleaf Family (Hydrophyllaceae)

JFMAMJJASOND

Carson's Phacelia has delicate purple and white flowers that fade to blue. The flower cluster continues to elongate as more flowers bloom; the older flowers produce a dense cluster of hairy seed pods.

 Dense clusters of ½″, bluish-purple, broad saucer-shaped flowers; each flower has 5 lobes with a dark purple midvein.

 Up to 3″, narrow, often covered with short white hair.

 Mountain brush and Pinyon/Juniper communities; low to moderate elevations.

 Western Utah counties; northwestern North America.

Other Names:
Threadleaf Phacelia

Second Species: Lanceleaf Phacelia *(Phacelia hastata)*, shown in the inset, is very common. It has dense clusters of purple to white cup-shaped flowers, with stamens that stick out beyond the corolla.

Up to 2′

161

STINKING HORSEMINT
(*Monardella odoratissima*)
Mint Family (Lamiaceae)

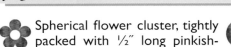

JFMAMJJASOND

Stinking Horsemint *is a clump-forming plant covered with buds and spherical clusters of purple flowers. It is a common late summer bloomer and has a strong fragrance.*

Up to 16"

 Spherical flower cluster, tightly packed with ½" long pinkish-purple flowers having 5 lobes.

 Up to 1½" long, lance shaped or elliptical, very fragrant.

 Mountain brush and forest communities; moderate to high elevations.

 All Utah counties; western US.

Monardella is named after Nicholas Monardes (1493–1588), a Spanish physician and botanist. *Odoratissima* means "fragrant" or "sweet smelling."

Other Names:
Mountain Monardella
Pennyroyal
Coyote Mint

162

WESTERN LARKSPUR
(*Delphinium occidentale*)
Buttercup Family (Ranunculaceae)

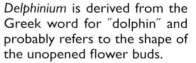

J F M A M J J A S O N D

Western Larkspur *appears in summer as a very tall spike of dark purple flowers on wildflower-covered hillsides. You can't miss it!*

 The inflorescence is a tall, dense, cylindrical spike of over thirty 1″ purple flowers.

 Up to 8″ wide, divided into three main lobes.

Mountain brush and forest communities; moderate to high elevations.

 Mountainous counties of Utah; northwestern North America.

 Delphinium is derived from the Greek word for ″dolphin″ and probably refers to the shape of the unopened flower buds.

Second Species: Low Larkspur (*Delphinium nuttallianum*), shown in the inset, is short and has mainly basal leaves. Its flower cluster is more open and less densely packed.

Up to 7′

163

MONKSHOOD
(*Aconitum columbianum*)
Buttercup Family (Ranunculaceae)

JFMAMJJASOND

Monkshood *is a tall plant topped with a long, open spike of deep purple flowers and large leaves. It is one of many members of the Buttercup family with intricate and unusually shaped flowers—the upper portion of the flower looks like a medieval monk's hood.*

Up to 5'

 Up to 2", 5 purple sepals looking like petals, usually just 2 petals hidden inside the hood.

 Up to 10" long and almost as broad, divided into 3–5 deeply cut lobes, each lobe divided into smaller lobes or teeth.

Meadow, grass/sedge, and open forest communities; moderate to high elevations.

 All Utah counties; western North America.

 Aconitum is Greek for "unconquerable poison." *Columbianum* refers to western North America. The whole plant, especially the roots and seeds, contains a poisonous alkaloid. Compare Monkshood with Western Larkspur on the previous page as they are sometimes confused for one another.

164

PURPLE VIRGINS-BOWER
(*Clematis occidentalis*)
Buttercup Family (Ranunculaceae)

JFMAMJJASOND

Purple Virgins-bower *is a woody, climbing vine with large purple flowers. Look for it along shady trails in the forest.*

 No petals, only four sepals that are up to 3″ long, purple or lavender, and spreading.

 Each leaf contains three leaflets that are lance or oval shaped.

 Moist woods or mountain brush communities.

 Mountainous counties of Utah; northwestern North America.

 Clematis is from the Greek word *klemma*, meaning "long, lithe branches." *Occidentalis* means "of the west."

Other Names:
Western Clematis

Second Species: Rocky Mountain Clematis (*Clematis columbiana*), shown in the inset, is not as high a climber, and its three leaflets are divided once or twice more into another set of three leaflets.

Up to 10′

165

LIONS-BEARD
(Clematis hirsutissima)
Buttercup Family (Ranunculaceae)

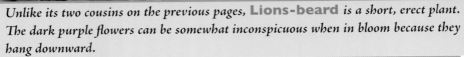

JFMAMJJASOND

Unlike its two cousins on the previous pages, Lions-beard is a short, erect plant. The dark purple flowers can be somewhat inconspicuous when in bloom because they hang downward.

Up to 28"

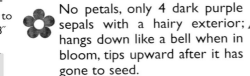

No petals, only 4 dark purple sepals with a hairy exterior; hangs down like a bell when in bloom, tips upward after it has gone to seed.

All of the Clematis species in this book form long, silvery plumes attached to the seeds, which catch the mountain breezes.

The leaves are finely divided, hairy, and a light-green color.

Mountain brush and forest communities; moderate to high elevations.

Most Utah counties; northwest North America.

Hirsutissima means "very hairy," in reference to the leaves and stems.

Other Names:

Sugarbowl

Hairy Clematis

Vase Vine

Leather Flower

ROCKY MOUNTAIN PENSTEMON
(Penstemon strictus)
Snapdragon Family (Scrophulariaceae)

J F M A M J J A S O N D

This **Penstemon** *can be found on the southern Wasatch Front. One easily reached place to look is just north of Cecret Lake in the Albion Basin. The bluish-purple flowers all stick straight out from the same side of the stem and fancifully look like a whale with its lower jaw open.*

 3–10 clusters; each cluster has 1–4 bluish-purple flowers with tufts of white hair on the staminode.

 Up to 4″, narrow, often folded (see inset).

 Mountain brush and forest communities; moderate to high elevations.

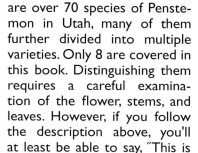 Wasatch Front, Uintahs, southeastern mountains; AZ, CO, MT, NM, WY.

 Strictus means "upright." There are over 70 species of Penstemon in Utah, many of them further divided into multiple varieties. Only 8 are covered in this book. Distinguishing them requires a careful examination of the flower, stems, and leaves. However, if you follow the description above, you'll at least be able to say, "This is *probably* the Rocky Mountain Penstemon."

Up to 3′

167

WHIPPLE'S PENSTEMON
(*Penstemon whippleanus*)
Snapdragon Family (Scrophulariaceae)

J F M A M J J A S O N D

Whipple's Penstemon *is very distinctive in its shape, color, and hairiness. The two pictures show both color phases. Look for it along trails at higher elevations.*

Up to 2′

4–6 clusters; each cluster has 1–5 wine-purple to dingy white flowers with tufts of white hair on the staminode and long white hair on the lower lip.

Up to 5″, lance shaped.

Forest, alpine meadow, and tundra communities; moderate to high elevations.

Most Utah counties; Rocky Mountains.

Whippleanus is named for Lt. Amiel Whipple (1817–63), who surveyed a southern route for a possible transcontinental railroad. Portions of this route later became Route 66.

168

LITTLECUP PENSTEMON
(Penstemon sepalulus)
Snapdragon Family (Scrophulariaceae)

J F M A M J J A S O N D

Littlecup Penstemon *is shrub-like with many spreading, slender branches containing clusters of pretty purple flowers. You can find it on the canyon walls of American Fork and Provo Canyons*

 3–15 clusters; each cluster has several purple flowers; the staminode is hairless.

 Up to 3″, very narrow.

 Talus slopes, rocky hillsides; low to moderate elevations.

 Southern Wasatch Front endemic; Utah, Wasatch, and Juab counties.

Up to 2 ½′

CORDROOT PENSTEMON
(*Penstemon montanus*)
Snapdragon Family (Scrophulariaceae)

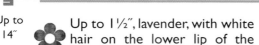

Cordroot Penstemon *is well adapted to rocky slopes and higher elevations. Its short stature, thick hairy leaves, and thick woody stem help it survive the wind, sun, and cold of the mountains. Look for a leafy mound, scattered with large lavender flowers.*

Up to 14″

 Up to 1½″, lavender, with white hair on the lower lip of the corolla.

Up to 2″, oval or lance shaped, serrated and hairy.

 Talus slopes, cliffs, limestone crevices; moderate to high elevations.

 Central and southern Wasatch Front; ID, MT, WY.

 This Penstemon is not seen as commonly as the others in this book, but the beauty of the flower, and the thick, woody stem (see inset) make it a Penstemon worth finding.

BLUE VIOLET
(Viola adunca)
Violet Family (Violaceae)

JFMAMJJASOND

Two purple violets are common on the Wasatch Front. Both have the typical violet shape, purple petals, and darker purple insect guidelines on the petals. Blue Violet *has a spur on the back with a slight hook on the end (not shown).*

 Up to 1″ long, purple (occasionally white) petals; the lower three petals are whitish at the base; some or all bearded with white hair.

 Up to 2½″, longer than they are broad, heart or kidney shaped, with shallow rounded teeth.

 Mountain brush and forest communities; low to high elevations.

 All Utah counties; northern and western US; Canada.

 Adunca means ″hooked″ and refers to the spur on the back side of the flower, which narrows and turns up.

Second Species: Bog Violet (*Viola nephrophylla*), shown in the inset, has only basal leaves and no hook on the end of the spur.

Up to 10″

171

Glossary

Anther: see stamen.

Banner: the upper, and usually largest petal of a Pea family flower. (See **Figure 1**.)

Basal: refers to something related to or located at the base of the plant. For example, the leaves attached at the base are "basal" leaves.

Bract: a reduced leaf at the base of the flower. The ribbed, overlapping, or leafy structures at the base of an Aster or Daisy are bracts (see Leafybract Aster). The colored "petals" of a Paintbrush are actually bracts, not petals.

Cauline: refers to something belonging to or located on the flowering stem of the plant. For example, the leaves that are attached to stem, above the base, are "cauline" leaves.

Calyx: this is the collective term for all the sepals. In **Figure 2**, the green tube at the base of the flower is called the "calyx tube." The pointy extensions are called the "calyx lobes." They represent the portions of the sepals that are fused and not fused, respectively.

Compound: with respect to leaves, this refers to similar leaflets joined together to make a larger structure, the leaf. **Figure 3** shows a Scarlet Gilia leaf composed of many tiny leaflets. (See also Umbel.)

Corolla: this is the collective term for all the petals. If a portion of the petals are fused together, the fused portion is called the "corolla tube," and each nonfused segment is called a "corolla lobe."

Disk Flowers: the flowers that form the central disk in Sunflower family flowers.

Inflorescence: the flowering part of the plant, which may be a cluster of flowers or a single flower.

Keel: the lower part of a Pea family flower, consisting of two petals fused together. (See **Figure 1**.)

Lance-shaped: shaped like the blade of a lance; longer than wide, with the widest point near the base. **Figure 4** shows the lance-shaped leaf of James' Chickweed. A reverse lance-shaped leaf would have its narrow end at the base of the leaf.

Lobe: a rounded segment of a plant part. (See also Calyx and Corolla.)

Nutlet: a section of the seeds of the Borage or Mint family.

Petal: an individual segment of the Corolla.

Pistil: the female organ of a flower, consisting of an ovary at the base, a style attached to the top of the ovary, and a stigma attached to the top of the style. **Figure 5** shows the ovoid ovary and stubby style (stigma not quite visible) of Elkweed.

Ray Flowers: the flowers that form the outer whorl of petals in Sunflower family flowers.

Sepal: an individual segment of the Calyx. (See **Figure 2**.)

Spatula-shaped: a term usually applied to the shape of a leaf that is widest near the rounded tip, and tapering to a narrower attachment point at the stem

Stamen: the male organ of a flower, consisting of a filament attached to the flower and an anther attached to the top of the filament. **Figure 5** shows an Elkweed flower with four thick filaments attached below the ovary and an anther atop each filament.

Staminode: a sterile, modified stamen. Look at the picture for Littlecup Penstemon. The white, tongue-like structure at the bottom of the corolla opening is a staminode.

Style: see Pistil.

Umbel: an inflorescence where the flower stems are attached to a central point. **Figure 6** shows small clusters of Western Sweet-cicely with long stems attached to a central point. If you look closely, you'll see that within the small clusters, the individual flowers are attached to another central point—the tip of the longer stem. This combination is a compound umbel.

Wings: the two side petals of a Pea family flower. (See **Figure 1**.)

Figure 1

Figure 2

Figure 3

Figure 4

Figure 5

Figure 6

REFERENCES

BOOKS

Blackwell, Laird G. 2005, *Great Basin Wildflowers: A Guide to Common Wildflowers of the High Deserts of Nevada, Utah, and Oregon*, ed 1. Morris Book Publishing, 281 pp.

Craighead, John J., Frank C. Craighead Jr., Ray J. Davis. 1991, *Peterson Field Guides: Rocky Mountain Wildflowers*, ed 2. Houghton Mifflin Company, 275 pp.

Harris, James G., and Melinda Woolf Harris. 2001, *Plant Identification Terminology: An Illustrated Glossary*, ed 2. Spring Lake Publishing, Spring Lake, UT, 216pp.

Shaw, Richard J. 1995, *Utah Wildflowers: A Field Guide to Northern and Central Mountains and Valleys*, ed 1. Utah State University Press, Logan, 218 pp.

Spellenberg, Richard. 2001, *National Audubon Society Field Guide to North American Wildflowers Western Region*, ed 2. Alfred A. Knopf, 862 pp.

Taylor, Ronald J. 1992, *Sagebrush Country: A Wildflower Sanctuary*, 2 ed. Mountain Press Publishing Company, Missoula, MT, 211 pp.

Welsh, S.L., N.D. Atwood, S. Goodrich, and L.C. Higgins. 2008, *A Utah Flora*, ed 4. BYU, Provo, UT, 1019 pp.

WEBSITES

California Plant Names: Latin and Greek Meanings and Derivations, Michael L. Charters, http://www.calflora.net/botanicalnames/

CalPhotos, http://calphotos.berkeley.edu/

eFloras, http://efloras.org/

Lady Bird Johnson Wildflower Center, http://www.wildflower.org/

Range Plants of Utah, Utah State University, http://extension.usu.edu/rangeplants/

Southwest Colorado Wildflowers, Ferns, and Trees, Al Schneider, http://www.swcoloradowildflowers.com/

USDA Plants Database, http://plants.usda.gov/

Utah Native Plant Society, http://www.unps.org/index.html

Utah Valley University Virtual Herbarium, http://herbarium.uvu.edu/Virtual/

Weeds and Wildflowers, http://www.rootcellar.us/wildflowers/contentt.htm

Wild Utah: Plant Index, http://www.wildutah.us/index_plant.html